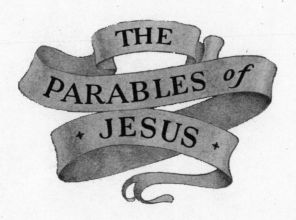

THE
PARABLES of
★ JESUS ★

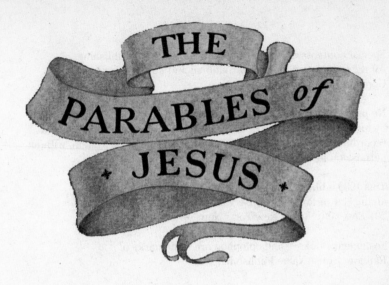

THE PARABLES *of* JESUS

S. PARKES CADMAN

ILLUSTRATED IN COLOR BY
N. C. WYETH

TESTAMENT BOOKS
NEW YORK

This 1999 edition is published by Testament Books,™
an imprint of Random House Value Publishing, Inc.,
201 East 50th Street, New York, New York 10022.

Testament Books™ and colophon are trademarks of
Random House Value Publishing, Inc.

Random House
New York • Toronto • London • Sydney • Auckland
http://www.randomhouse.com/

Printed and bound in the United States of America

*A CIP catalog record for this book is available from the Library of
Congress.*

The Parables of Jesus / by S. Parkes Cadman / illustrated by N. C. Wyeth /
reprint of the edition of 1931, published by David McKay
ISBN 0-517-20546-7

8 7 6 5 4 3 2

CONTENTS

CONTENTS

LIST OF ILLUSTRATIONS
(Color section follows page 60)

———————

FOREWORD

Dr. A. B. Bruce finds in the Gospels thirty-three parables and eight parable germs which he classifies as didactic, evangelic, and prophetic. Dr. A. Jülicher reckons fifty-three, and distributes them into twenty-one parables proper, twenty-eight similitudes and four example stories. Dr. G. Stanley Hall separates these into twenty-eight comparison parables, twenty-one true parables, and four illustrative narratives. The purpose of this book is best served by their three-fold grouping as *Parables of the Kingdom; Parables showing the Grace of God;* and *Parables of Moral Instruction and Warning.* These number approximately thirty-three, but some are here taken in pairs, since, as in the parables of "The Hidden Treasure" and "The Pearl of Great Price," or those of "The Talents" and "The Pounds," they present the same truth under different forms. The treatment given them, illuminated as it is by the exquisite art of Mr. Wyeth, is intended for the general reader. If it introduces the peerless teachings of these Divine stories to the larger public, the aim of this volume will have been gained.

January Twenty-fourth,
1931

S. Parkes Cadman.

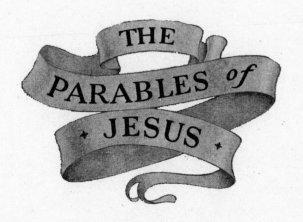

CHAPTER I
THE DAWN OF GOD'S DAY FOR THE WORLD

Chapter I

THE DAWN OF GOD'S DAY FOR THE WORLD

A GLAD confident morning for humanity broke upon its prolonged night when "Jesus came into Galilee, preaching the gospel of God, and saying, The time is fulfilled, and the kingdom of God is at hand: repent ye, and believe in the gospel."[1] The radiance of this oncoming day is clearly seen in the four Evangels which portray Jesus in a threefold light, as *the Master*, whose precepts centered on His disciples; *the Evangelist*, who went about doing good, and preaching to the neglected folk of Palestine the Gospel of His Kingdom; and *the Prophet*, who proclaimed anew with startling authority the universal moral government of God. The parables of Jesus contain the marrow of His teaching, and unfold the love, justice and compassion which animated His redemptive mission. For if the four Gospels, as the noblest religious documents extant, may be compared to a massive ring of gold, after the pattern of the one described in Robert Browning's poem, "The Ring and the Book," of "rondure

---

[1] St. Mark 1 : 14, 15.

brave," and "lilied loveliness"; surely the Master's parables are comparable to so many gems "of purest ray serene" adorning that ring. He is the Light of the world, and nowhere does His light shine with more luster than through the beautiful prismatic rays of these sayings.[1] They are one of Heaven's choicest gifts, bestowed in sublime yet simple forms, which transmit the profoundest wisdom by means of stories intimately concerned with the normal existence of those who heard them. Jesus employed the old metaphors, images and phraseologies of everyday life and conversation because the technical language of thinkers and theologians was unsuited to His purpose. He uttered the current speech of the plain folk in whom His soul delighted. What He said was redolent of the ancient East: of its homes, farmsteads, villages and cities. He had nothing more than a manger in a stable, a carpenter's tools, a rustic gathering on the hillside— *and His own creative Personality*. With these he overcame the bitterest opposition, and set in motion the mightiest moral revolution which has upraised mankind. His appeal was not to schools of learning or of criticism, but to man as man, and to man's felt needs.

He dealt broadly with those religious ideas of the Jews which stand out against a background of eternity

[1] Cf. A. B. Bruce: *The Parabolic Teaching of Christ*, pp. 3–4.

and interwove their laws, beliefs, literatures and customs into His parables. Their concrete verities were enforced by His marvellous insight, keen observation and infinite range of feeling. A hallowed idealism mellowed His reflections; His perspectives of life were comprehensive, including things seen and unseen, and separating actual from fictitious values. Not a few of His stories are aromatic with the dewy scents of His home in the Galilean hills. They visualize a fair, sweet, joyous landscape; the music of its birds, the green of its trees, the sound of its rippling waters; a landscape crowded with beautiful sceneries, and the breath of flowers, the golden waves of harvest, the gleaming of stars on moving seas. Other stories reflect the grandeur of His stormier moods, when with words that burned, He rebuked the habitual insolence of oppressors, hypocrites and sycophants who trampled on the heart of a great nation. Creeds from which every virtue had long since vanished aroused His righteous indignation, and this broke forth in utterances which stand out as beacons of warning against the seductive sins of pride and obstinacy.

His parables freed religion from its restrictive elements by emphasizing the right of every seeker after God to immediate fellowship with Him. The "Living Water" symbolizing that fellowship flowed through them in soul refreshing streams. They were hailed with gratitude by men and women weary of vain traditions and legal niceties. They blazed the trail for those advocates of Christianity who afterwards marched to the conquests of the Cross. They anticipated its triumphs over the brilliant but decadent Paganism of the Greco-Roman Empire. They shattered the bondage of a bigoted orthodoxy based upon outworn assumptions and codes. Popular ideas of religion were rescued from the rigid rules and far-fetched theories of ecclesiasticism and transferred to a realm of inwardness and power. In these parables we can discern the unconquerable democracy of Christ's Christianity as a manifestation of redeeming love in which the whole human race is included. By them the peoples of East and West are made aware of God's fatherly love, transcendent grace, everlasting mercy, and inerrant justice.

We have heard of Jesus as the anointed Prophet, Priest and King of men. May we not glimpse Him in His teaching ministry as their Divine Poet? For here He overcomes the sad incompetence of human speech to convey the loftiest verities, and causes them to enter through the lowliest doors of homely similes. Moreover, what the parables did for the first and subsequent centuries they can do for the twentieth. They still consist of Christ's woven breath. The lambent flame of His glorious soul still glows undiminished in them.

The parable proper may be defined as a narration of well known scenes or events in human life and its surroundings for the purposes of giving them a moral or religious application. Occasionally it took shape in action, as in the case of Isaiah, who paraded the streets of Jerusalem, half clad, to shame the peace made by Judah with Egypt.[1] By adopting the parable, Jesus sanctioned an ageless method of instruction prevalent in the Orient from the Yang-tse-Kiang in China to the Ganges in India, and westward as far as the Jordan Valley. The inhabitants of this vast territory have always thought, felt and spoken in picturesque comparisons and similitudes; interpreting the visible by the invisible, and the peculiar by the common. Their poets and romancers, while as a rule careful to keep within the bounds of actual experience, exercised a vivid imagination to stress an incident or enforce a moral. Their abuse of the parabolic method, however, confined men's aspirations, and encouraged the fatalism which thwarts Oriental life and action. For a better though quite sparing use of that method, we turn to the Old Testament prophets; but for its divine use we hasten to the Christ who is the Saviour of the world.

[1] Isaiah 20 : 1–6.

He invested the parable with its imperishable worth and made it the golden key to the door of Truth's sanctuary.

Enough has perhaps been said to enable us to glimpse the far reaching hinterlands of poetry, dream and vision awaiting our Lord's entrance upon His ministry. St. John the Baptist had already stung the conscience of the Jewish people by his fearless reminder that the ax was "laid unto the root of the trees," and that "every tree which bringeth not forth good fruit is hewn down and cast into the fire."[1] This note gave Jesus the cue for His opening message of the Sermon on the Mount, which was steeped in the ethic and the piety of Old Testament psalmists and seers, and stressed the prior claims of justice and truth over rituals and ordinances. For the moment decorum repressed and policy concealed the rising animosity of the Temple officials and custodians of the law against this youthful usurper of their privileges. Meanwhile, the crowds which had heard with avidity the Master's earlier words fell away from Him rather than comply with His demand for a righteousness exceeding that of the Scribes and Pharisees. This combination of official fury and intolerance with the shallowness of the populace prompted Christ's emphasis on parables. He

[1] St. Matthew 3 : 7–12.

used them as a practiced speaker uses the art of illus-
tration in addressing a promiscuous audience. As the
unsetting sun of the Kingdom of Heaven, He was indifferent to the applause and emoluments of earth.
From the day of His baptism in the wilderness to that
of His offering at Calvary, it was His engrossing purpose to focus the Gospel of His Incarnation. But this
could not be done, nor the Kingdom's foundation be
firmly laid, until He had secured convinced assent to
His message. So He framed it, not only for those who
hated Him, nor for the remnant who heeded Him, but
for all who listened to think for themselves, and whose
decision to obey as well as hearken ultimately trans-
formed the religious outlook of the world.

It should be understood that the parables of Jesus
were not only models of the literary art. To be sure,
they used

> "The simplest sights we met—
> The Sower flinging seed on loam and rock;
> The darnel in the wheat; the mustard tree
> That hath its seed so little, and its boughs
> Wide-spreading; and the wandering sheep; and nets
> Shot in the wimpled waters,—drawing forth
> Great fish and small."[1]

These and a hundred such sights seen by men daily,
though seldom seen aright, were Christ's pictures from

[1] Sir Edwin Arnold: *The Light of the World.*

the pages of life. But He gave them a unique spiritual significance, enhanced by their extraordinary beauty of allusion, and by His fellowship with God, Man and Nature.

The interest of the parables is further heightened by the fact that they constitute the larger part of Christ's recorded teaching. The principles embodied in them with such vividness and fascination, and the experiences created by them in universal Christendom, are heirlooms which those who love Christ, and would know Him better, cannot prize too highly.

CHAPTER II
THE PARABLES OF THE KINGDOM

I. THE PARABLE OF THE SOWER

"And He spake to them many things in parables, saying, Behold, the sower went forth to sow; and as he sowed, some seeds fell by the wayside, and the birds came and devoured them: and others fell upon the rocky places, where they had not much earth: and straightway they sprang up, because they had no deepness of earth: and when the sun was risen, they were scorched; and because they had no root they withered away. And others fell upon the thorns; and the thorns grew up and choked them: and others fell upon the good ground, and yielded fruit, some a hundredfold, some sixty, some thirty. He that hath ears to hear, let him hear."

St. Matthew 13 : 3-9.

Chapter II

THE PARABLES OF THE KINGDOM

I

THE parables of the Kingdom are steeped in the Master's love for the secrets of the field, the sights of the highway and the panorama of life. This story of the Sower is not only an example of His attachment to God's good world: it also serves as an admirable introduction to the parables that follow it. We may imagine for ourselves the circumstances evoking it. Jesus leaves the house in which He is staying, and takes His seat in the boat anchored near the shore on which stood His friends, the fishermen and tillers of the soil. The Lake whose waters shone like a silver shield, its encompassing hills and valleys, the cattle grazing in the pastures, and the ploughmen busy on the lowlands, are for Him sacramental tokens of His Father's care for man and beast. The farmer casting His seed into the earth is increasing, not wasting it, for he does so confident that he will reap a harvest. His work at once suggests to Jesus His experience as a Teacher. For He too had seed which must be sown, and He was eager to scatter it abroad. So it was incumbent upon Him to be about His Father's business, whether others regarded Him seriously or not. He flung to the winds the prudence which overreaches itself; drove the plough of His mandates through every makeshift and pretense; broke up the fallow ground of hardened hearts and superficial moralities.

Notwithstanding disappointments ahead, He never yielded to gloom or depression. No opposition, however subtle or avowed, could daunt Him. When the dark shadow of the Cross fell athwart His path, He was still sowing on every kind of soil that human hearts contained: some hard and stony with prejudice and hate; some fertile and responsive with loyalty and obedience. As God's tireless husbandman, He cast His seed into the soul of Judas the betrayer as liberally as into the soul of St. John the beloved disciple. Nor did He cease from sowing, until the crimson rain of His sacrificial love so fertilized the seed that it bore fruit, and whitened unto an everlasting harvest.

That stirring novel, "Giants in the Earth," is an enlightening commentary on this parable. The fierce struggle of its Norwegian immigrants against loneliness, homesickness, severe winters, desperate sickness and recurrent plagues of locusts, emphasizes the meaning of the Master's words. Their indomitable courage and tenacity reflect His spirit. That spirit has been vindicated by the triumphs of His Kingdom. The deathless life of its divine Author was in it from the first, and shall be in it to the end. Encased in their seeming houses of death, coffered in dusty barns and outbuildings, forlorn as ashes, shrivelled and scentless, the dry seeds awake at Spring's caress; that from them flowers by the million may leap, and stately forests, or expansive plains covered with ripe corn, emerge for the service of man. Jesus likewise knew that His words were "spirit and life," having in them the dynamic force to create a new world.

Yet neither the greatest of Sowers nor the best of seeds can produce good crops without suitable soil. The Master names six varieties, three alike decidedly inferior; another three varying in their yielding capacity. The wayside soil symbolizes those who refuse to evaluate life aright. *Seeing*, they do not see; *hearing*, they do not understand. The rocky soil symbolizes superficial souls who never penetrate below the surface of thinking and living, and have no depth of nature in which the truth can strike and take hold. The thorny soil symbolizes the conflicting interests of the world which is "too much with us, late and soon," the "getting and spending" of which "lay waste our powers." Even the good ground varies in its fruitfulness. Yet

whether this is thirty, sixty or a hundredfold, Jesus is
chiefly concerned that none should allow the poison of
secularism to stifle the soul or to petrify its nobler aspirations. John Masefield has given us the gist of this
parable in the following stanzas, taken from his poem,
"The Everlasting Mercy"—

> "O Christ who holds the open gate,
> O Christ who drives the furrow straight,
> O Christ, the plough, O Christ, the laughter
> Of holy white birds flying after,
> Lo, all my heart's field red and torn,
> And Thou wilt bring the young green corn,
> The young green corn divinely springing,
> The young green corn for ever singing;
> And when the field is fresh and fair
> Thy blessèd feet shall glitter there,
> And we will walk the weeded field,
> And tell the golden harvest's yield,
> The corn that makes the holy bread
> By which the soul of man is fed,
> The holy bread, the food unpriced,
> Thy everlasting mercy, Christ."

II. THE PARABLE OF THE TARES

"Another parable set he before them, saying, The Kingdom of heaven is likened unto a man that sowed good seed in his field: but while men slept, his enemy came and sowed tares also among the wheat, and went away. But when the blade sprang up and brought forth fruit, then appeared the tares also. And the servants of the householder came and said unto him, Sir, didst thou not sow good seed in thy field? whence then hath it tares? And he said unto them, An enemy hath done this. And the servants say unto him, Wilt thou then that we go and gather them up? But he saith, Nay; lest haply while ye gather up the tares, ye root up the wheat with them. Let both grow together until the harvest: and in the time of the harvest I will say to the reapers, Gather up first the tares, and bind them in bundles to burn them; but gather the wheat into my barn."

St. Matthew 13 : 24–30.

II

THE parable of the Tares, while colored by Christ's close affiliation with Nature, was prompted by His knowledge of the human heart's utmost recesses. The allusions of the narrative conform with the circumstances it relates. Today, as in His time, malicious Arabs mutilate a neighboring farmer's olive trees or set fire to his hay stacks. The darnel, as the parable's particular weed is called, still grows in the wheat, and can scarcely be distinguished from it during their earlier stages. By the time they have reached maturity, their roots are so interlaced that the one cannot be plucked up without injuring the other. But happily the wheat grows higher than the tares, and this enables the reaper to gather his harvest without touching the tares. The cry: "Raise your sickles!" is often heard in Palestine's fields when the laborers, absorbed in their task, forget to cut above the darnel nestling under the wheat. After the reaping is finished the darnel is ploughed out, raked into bundles and burnt.

So much for an agricultural scene of the usual kind, which supplies Jesus with material for a striking comparison. But its interpretation is by no means easy.

31

Nor does the one contained in the context (13 : 36–43), although attributed to our Lord Himself, accord with His temper or with the general tenor of His teaching. Its stilted style, excessive details, use of apocalyptic imageries and of certain metaphors and titles, indicate that this explanatory passage is probably a later addition to the narrative, and therefore secondary in character. Some New Testament scholars have suggested that the parable itself was born in the circles of the early Church, when she was too feeble or too acquiescent to tackle the gross evils which beset her. Other scholars accept the parable as Christ's utterance, but differ concerning its meaning. The field has been compared to the Church, and again to the world; the tares, to backslidden saints, and also to avowed sinners. Perhaps the most direct explanation is that so long as sin exists in the world it is sure to infect the Church, and impede the Kingdom's progress. A spiritual organization which must keep in touch with mundane affairs cannot be wholly immune from their contagion. And if the tares spring up in her wheat, the Church is obligated to get rid of them. Yet her judgments begin and end with herself; God alone decrees the final destiny of His own creation.[1]

Even the casual reader may perceive that the par-

[1] Cf. I Corinthians 5 : 9–13.

able predicts the approach of a crucial hour in which all souls shall be known for what they are. Wheat will then be wheat, tares will be tares, and neither adroit pretenses nor fervent protests can confuse the one with the other. This is the consummation of earth's chequered story of good and evil: of the sowing and the reaping which fulfil the purpose of God's Kingdom. Aware that "things are what they are," and that "the consequences will be what they will be," the Kingdom's servants do not have to permit hypocrisy in its adherents, any more than they have to countenance flagrant wickedness beyond its borders. Assuredly those who must themselves appear before Heaven's tribunal cannot assume its judicial functions. It is enough for us to know that men and women to whom the Kingdom is dear beyond all else have no reason to fear, while those who wilfully impede its progress by sowing tares in the wheat ought to fear.

III. THE PARABLES OF THE MUSTARD SEED AND THE LEAVEN

(A) "Another parable set he before them, saying, The kingdom of heaven is like unto a grain of mustard seed, which a man took, and sowed in his field, which indeed is less than all seeds; but when it is grown, it is greater than the herbs, and becometh a tree, so that the birds of the heaven come and lodge in the branches thereof.

(B) "Another parable spake he unto them; The kingdom of heaven is like unto leaven, which a woman took, and hid in three measures of meal, till it was all leavened."

St. Matthew 13 : 31–33.

34

III

(A) The saying "as small as a grain of mustard seed" was so proverbial among the Jews that it expressed for them the irreducible minimum of size. This is its meaning here and elsewhere in the words of Jesus. It is also found in the Koran and the Talmud· St. Matthew's Gospel gives a more satisfactory report of the parable before us than those of St. Mark and St. Luke. The Master selected the black mustard plant to illustrate the Kingdom's advance from a small beginning to a great end, and it is characteristic that He should stress its modest rise and progress far more than its stupendous destiny. Moreover, there is nothing insipid about mustard, neither is there anything neutral about the Kingdom's ideals. They are distinctive, unmistakable: sharply divisive between sacrificial servants of God and flesh worshippers who are lovers of themselves. Consider also that a single seed, entirely apart from hosts of similar seed, contains within itself the vitality achieving such marvellous results. Further, the birds sheltering in the mustard plant and feeding on its fruit reminded Jesus of nations yet unborn which should enjoy the Kingdom's protecting strength and benediction.

(B) As a boy He often heard the sound of His mother at the mill grinding the corn for the family's daily food, and saw her inserting in the meal the leaven which leavened the whole measure. Yet the adverse view of leaven seemed to forbid its metaphorical use as a type of moral energy. Under the Jewish law no leaven was allowed in offerings laid upon the altar. Cora Harris wittily observes that when St. Paul said: "a little leaven leaveneth the whole lump," "he was warning the Corinthian Christians against one of their prominent members whose morals had fermented." Despite this prejudice, the Christ who came to make all things new likened His life and teachings to the leaven's permeating processes. Through their pervasive influence the Kingdom spreads apace and prospers by means of an indwelling vitality.

The comparisons of these parables are taken at first hand from the Master's surroundings, and they subserve His purpose in a twofold manner. The first teaches that God's Kingdom shall increase as a visible society; the second, that it will make itself felt as an ever growing moral force. The one predicts the *extensive*, the other, the *intensive* development of the Divine Society. The gigantic tree that grew from the solitary mustard seed symbolizes the historical conditions of the Kingdom's expansion. The leaven which leavened all the meal symbolizes the Kingdom's silent elements of truth and righteousness.

You may ask if Christ's optimistic forecast has been verified. The answer is found after making every allowance in the contrast between the civilization of the Roman Empire under whose dominion Jesus lived and died, and that of the modern nations of North America and of Europe. The genesis of His mission seemed less than nothing to grave doctors of the law at Jerusalem or the powerful proconsuls of Cæsar Augustus. Yet these potentates have passed forever, while Jesus remains as the Light of life and the Hope of men. Well might St. Paul exclaim: "God chose the foolish things of the world, that He might put to shame them that are wise, and . . . the weak things of the world, that He might put to shame the things that are strong . . . and the things that are not, that He might bring to nought the things that are."[1] These magnificent paradoxes chide our fears for the Kingdom's future, and confirm our faith in its triumph over the limitless arrogance, selfishness and vanity of its foes. For God spoke, and the world was! Christ spoke, and that world was reborn! In Him "Mercy and truth are met together; Righteousness and peace have kissed each other."[2]

[1] I Corinthians 1 : 26-28.   [2] Psalms 85 : 10.

IV. THE PARABLES OF THE HIDDEN TREASURE AND THE PEARL OF GREAT PRICE

(A) "The kingdom of heaven is like unto a treasure hidden in the field; which a man found, and hid; and in his joy he goeth and selleth all that he hath, and buyeth that field.

(B) "Again, the kingdom of heaven is like unto a man that is a merchant seeking goodly pearls: and having found one pearl of great price, he went and sold all that he had, and bought it."

St. Matthew 13 : 44-46.

IV

THESE exquisite miniatures of "The Hidden Treasure" and "The Pearl" occupy a small corner in St. Matthew's spacious Gospel; but both are superb examples of their Divine Artist's genius for displaying the exhaustless riches of the Kingdom. Taken from different spheres of activity, the two parables complement each other, and illustrate those spiritual treasures of purity, joy, peace and blessedness which are "above all we can ask or think." Their implication is that, cost what they may, the treasures must be ours. No other ideals of life and action vie with those the Treasure and the Pearl make manifest. The brave pioneers now engaged in climbing the Himalayan peaks tell us that even the Alps are easy compared with the conquest of Kanchinjanga, and especially mighty Everest. So is it concerning the towering heights of character which Jesus sets before us. They dominate the spiritual landscape with a majestic holiness before which the stars themselves are impure: heights inaccessible to our unaided earth-bound spirits. Yet they have been scaled, and those whose devotion doubles their energy, and gives birth to heroic action, may repeat the achievement.

(A) Hiding treasure is a habit in every disturbed land, and in those of the East it is chronic. Two

Moguls of India, Akbar and Jahanger, accumulated buried money equal to three billion dollars in American currency: a colossal amount swollen by huge quantities of bullion and jewels. Ancient Roman law allowed the discoverer of such treasure one half its value. But the man in the first of the two parables decided to evade the law, and seize the whole amount. Watch him digging the soil in a field he does not own, and probably regretting his toilsome lot. Just then his pick strikes an old wine jar carefully sealed. He breaks the seal, and out pours a stream of gold and silver coins. He looks and acts like one demented. Surely the wealth at his feet cannot be real. Nevertheless, it is; and he realizes he is rich beyond the dreams of avarice. Casting a hasty glance around to assure himself that no one observes him, he conceals his finding, hastens to sell all his possessions in order to purchase the field, and thus legalizes his claim to the money.

(B) The second parable likens the Kingdom's endowments to a pearl of great price: the favorite jewel of Eastern merchants because of its unique luster and supposedly occult properties. Its chaste splendors so impressed the author of the Book of Revelation that he described the great gateways into the City of God as twelve single pearls.[1] Note that the merchant of

---

[1] Revelation 21 : 21.

the narrative did not *find* his pearl; he *bought* it. Having seen it, he never rested until this queen of precious stones was his. His entire stock in trade was cheerfully sacrificed for the prize which outshone them all. Better own the Koh-i-noor than a bagful of inferior jewels.

Such comparisons are lucidity itself. They demonstrate that whatever the Kingdom requires should be freely surrendered. But many who concede its right to every service they can pay hesitate when its claims are presented. They retreat before the Master's mandate: "He that loveth father or mother more than me is not worthy of me; . . . and he that doth not take his cross and follow after me, is not worthy of me. He that findeth his life shall lose it; and he that loseth his life for my sake shall find it."[1] Yet this is the true Gospel and sufficient creed which has built the Kingdom's bulwarks over against the very doors of Hell and Death. Men and women are redeemed, under God, by resolute defenders of His cause who reckon all else refuse so that they may gain Christ, and inherit in Him the unsearchable riches of love, justice and brotherhood symbolized by these parables. Those who accept their mandate shall stand at God's right hand when earth's wealth and whatever it can procure are as though they had never been.

[1] St. Matthew 10 : 37–39.

V. THE PARABLE OF THE DRAG-NET

"Again, the kingdom of heaven is like unto a net, that was cast into the sea, and gathered of every kind: which, when it was filled, they drew up on the beach; and they sat down, and gathered the good into vessels, but the bad they cast away. So shall it be in the end of the world: the angels shall come forth, and sever the wicked from among the righteous, and shall cast them into the furnace of fire: there shall be the weeping and the gnashing of teeth."

St. Matthew 13 : 47–50.

V

St. Matthew closes his great thirteenth chapter of parables with a story located on Lake Galilee's western shore. This was Palestine's fishing ground, furnishing considerable food supplies, and having at least twenty edible species of fish in its sunny shoals. The net referred to in the parable was a "djarf arabe" or drag-net, and it is used today by the Cornish fishermen of England, who call it the seine. This net is a long, closely woven band, the upper and lower parts of which are weighted to sweep the shallows, in which respect it differs from the throw net, which was intended for deep water fishing. Habakkuk refers to both kinds in the passage: "He catcheth them in his net, and gathereth them in his drag."[1] The one end of the drag-net is taken out by a group of wading fishermen, while another group stays in the boat near the land, until the net encloses whatever is between them; then they haul it in, and every sort of fish, good, bad or indifferent, is drawn shoreward. Few sights are more exciting than the pulling in of the drag-net. The floats on the shallows begin to bob, the cords attached

[1] Habakkuk 1 : 15.

43

to each end of the net tighten, the waters boil as the seething masses of entangled fish leap and struggle, the eager spectators crowd around until the haul is completed; after which the edible fish are put into vessels and the worthless ones thrown aside.

Here the original parable probably ended; in which case verses forty-nine and fifty should be regarded as the additions of an ambitious scribe who placed his own construction on the Master's words. It is as though Jesus said: "I see before me a given expanse of life's sea into which the Kingdom's drag-net is cast. It includes within its scope not only living men and women, but also their ideals and conceptions. Those who are in the net are caught and appraised: *not those who are in the sea.*" Whoever among professed Christians is inferior in motive and aim, or whatever in them is unfit for the Kingdom's mission to mankind, must be rejected. God's spokesmen can be none other than the pure in heart, whose words and deeds exhibit spiritual regeneration in concrete forms.

Evidently being in the net does not guarantee the fine quality of the catch. Character alone determines that. Indifferent Christians who harbor what is mean and base will not escape its haul any more than sincere and earnest believers. The parable also assures us that the Lord of the Kingdom will presently determine the faith and works, not only of individuals but of baptized Christendom, its nations and institutions. Their trial is not invariably postponed to the Great Assize. It proceeds continuously in history lest evil should overcome good. The God who loves righteousness and hates iniquity casts His drag-net into humanity's tempestuous ocean, and what He finds there at deadly issue with His will must be judged accordingly. That net brought to the surface of the World War's red flood monstrosities so ferocious and futile that even secular minds denounced them as the spawn of the pit. The paramount obligation of the Kingdom's adherents is their extermination. For should they be permitted to exist, the next cast of the drag-net may haul in our boasted civilization as hopelessly degenerate; fit for nothing but to be discarded and trodden down.

VI. THE PARABLE OF THE SEED GROWING SECRETLY

"And he said, So is the kingdom of God, as if a man should cast seed upon the earth; and should sleep and rise night and day, and the seed should spring up and grow, he knoweth not how. The earth beareth fruit of herself; first the blade, then the ear, then the full grain in the ear. But when the fruit is ripe, straightway he putteth forth the sickle, because the harvest is come."

St. Mark 4 : 26–29.

VI

THIS parable, which is the last of the series dealing directly with the Kingdom, is recorded only by St. Mark, the value of whose Gospel it enhances by the single phrase: "the earth beareth fruit of herself." Correctly translated, it should read: "the earth beareth fruit *automatically*." The Greek term Jesus used was "automatos," which has the significance of the English rendition, "automatic." The word also occurs in Leviticus 25 : 5, where it refers to the harvest which takes care of itself during the Sabbatical Year; and in Acts 12 : 10, where it shows that the iron gate of St. Peter's prison at Jerusalem opened of its own accord to release him. Jesus does not linger on the sowing of the seed or the risks of its growth. These He describes elsewhere. But He calls our attention to the frequently forgotten fact that, after all, the farmer's intervention is needed only at the beginning and the end of the process. During the long interval between the sowing and the reaping the seed safeguards itself. Its sprouting, maturing and fructifying are inherent and spontaneous. The miracle of its growth is Nature's sole business. She creates those mysterious renewals of

life and fecundity which the calendar's seasons regis-
ter.   To her belongs the credit of Winter's rest period,
Spring's resurrection, Summer's luxuriance and Au-
tumn's fruitfulness.   Assured of her secret help, the
husbandman can wait patiently for the early and the
later rains.   Because he is aware of her God-directed
workings he sleeps, wakes and pursues his daily course.
While he prepares for the harvest he watches his crops
repeating this annual marvel.   Knowing that after
the blade will come the ear, then the full kernel in the
ear, he has no qualms.   When the ripe grain rustles
in the breeze he sends forth the reapers, singing their
song of the corn, to gather it in.

In his discourses Epictetus gives an interesting
parallel to this parable. "Fruit grows thus: The seed
must be buried for some time, be hid, grow secretly,
that it may come to perfection . . . Let the root
grow, then acquire the first joint, then the second,
then the third.   In this manner the fruit will naturally
force its way out."   Of course it will, for should it
cease to do so, farmers may as well throw their seed
into the crater of an active volcano as sow it on the
richest soil.   Fortunately for us all, Nature does not
lie.   Unlike man, she refuses to waste her energies for
incomplete or detrimental results.   Her trustworthi-
ness is the basis of his confident toil.

Dr. Newton Davies has expounded the essential meaning of the parable in "The Abingdon Bible Commentary"; a book which deserves a place in every man's library. "Jesus here seeks to point out, first, that there is a mysterious, divine element working in spiritual growth as well as in natural growth; and second, that in the spiritual realm one must wait on God's time."[1] It is the duty of parents, teachers and preachers to prepare the soil, sow the right kind of seed, and keep on sowing it. They must imitate the farmer by cultivating that patience of hope which follows the labor of love. The God who will not allow earth's seed time and harvest to fail exercises ultimate control over the devices and desires of human hearts. Those who share the work of their Lord for the Kingdom should also share His optimism. He did not despair of mankind, neither should we. One is not surprised that St. Mark inserted this encouraging parable in the Evangel which he wrote for the persecuted Church at Rome. Its emperors could slay the sowers and the reapers, but they could not sterilize the seed. Neither can the incipient or actual materialists of our day. Once we have sown it Heaven will cause it to bear fruit.

[1] p. 1006.

Chapter III
Parables Illustrating the Grace of God

I. THE PARABLE OF THE TWO DEBTORS

"And Jesus answering said unto him, Simon, I have somewhat to say unto thee. And he saith, Teacher, say on. A certain lender had two debtors: the one owed five hundred shillings, and the other fifty. When they had not wherewith to pay, he forgave them both. Which of them therefore will love him most? Simon answered and said, He, I suppose, to whom he forgave the most. And he said unto him, Thou hast rightly judged. And turning to the woman, he said unto Simon, Seest thou this woman? I entered into thy house, thou gavest me no water for my feet: but she hath wetted my feet with her tears, and wiped them with her hair. Thou gavest me no kiss: but she, since the time I came in, hath not ceased to kiss my feet. My head with oil thou didst not anoint: but she hath anointed my feet with ointment. Wherefore I say unto thee, Her sins, which are many, are forgiven; for she loved much: but to whom little is forgiven, the same loveth little."

St. Luke 7 : 40–47.

Chapter III

PARABLES ILLUSTRATING THE GRACE OF GOD

I

JESUS was not accustomed to courtesy from the Pharisees. As a sect, they were not without surface merits. But they loved to pose as the God appointed rulers of the dumb masses. Their assumptions were the more repellent because they were paraded in the guise of sanctimonious piety. Their intrusive recti- tude was fatally deficient in that saving quality of common sense which fosters a healthy contempt for trivialities and pretensions. Yet we are not to suppose they resembled peas in a pod. There were Pharisees *and* Pharisees, and Simon, from whose house Jesus transmitted "The Parable of the Two Debtors" to the world, was evidently a man of broader views than the majority of his caste. He was so curious about the Master that his curiosity overcame his prejudice. For Jesus had received the greatest distinction that could be given Him: He was openly acclaimed as a prophet, and confessedly His personality attracted friend and foe. Unlike John the Baptist, He was not a recluse nor an ascetic. He did not shun the crowds nor decline their hospitality. So Simon invited this gifted young Galilean to dine with him, just as modern "lion hunters" of both sexes invite celebrities or eccentric geniuses. Of course it would never do to make too much of Jesus. He had to be kept in His place, and not be allowed to forget that He was feasting with the best people of Magdala. After all, He was only a carpenter, and of all places—from Nazareth; to be received with scant ceremony, and speedily dismissed when Simon had discovered the secret of His popularity.

But it was a day of surprises for the Pharisee. He reckoned without his guest, and his gravest miscalculation was caused by the unexpected entrance of a notorious courtesan of the town. No sooner did she learn that Jesus was in Simon's house, than she thrust herself upon the self-complacent and patronizing company. Heedless of their haughty scorn and astonished mutterings, the abused, abandoned woman knelt behind the Master as He sat at meat; bathed with her tears His feet for which Simon had omitted to offer Him the customary water; dried them with her hair, and anointed them with the precious ointment she had procured for that purpose.

The parable evoked by this strange interruption is

embedded in its setting like a crystal in amber. The conclusion forced upon Simon by Christ's question as to which of the two debtors mentioned would love their creditor most was obviously true. The one to whom the larger obligation was remitted would feel correspondingly grateful. But how did the comparison apply to the penitent woman, and also to those present, specifically to Simon? Straitlaced precisians of the time ostracized her sex, and consigned her calamitous calling to the devil. What followed reveals the noble humanitarianism of St. Luke's Gospel, and the Master's deep reverence for womanhood. The Evangelist's sensitive respect for this destitute soul forbade the mention of her name. The Divine Love Jesus diffused throughout the incident not only canceled her sin; it concealed her identity.

At this juncture He turned the tables on His neglectful host. It is as though He had said to Simon: "You are right in your estimate of this woman. Nevertheless, she is nearer Heaven in her penitence than you are in your fastidious orthodoxy. Her sins have been forgiven for the sake of her sorrow, her faith and her service. You imagine that since I have not spurned her, I am no prophet. But my very acceptance of her homage is a signal proof of my Divine commission. The measure of her pardon is determined by the measure of her love. Her conscious restoration releases in her heart love's purifying grace. She has greatly ventured; she is greatly forgiven. But what about you, Simon? By the same token, you are forgiven little because you love little."

The proud Pharisee made no reply. In fact, he had none to make. Overwhelmed by what they had witnessed, his guests silently withdrew. The woman, recreated and blessed in her new found peace, went out aware that contact with Jesus had for her all the values of her Heavenly Father's changeless mercy. Modern Simons, reminiscent of the French duchess who remarked that God would think twice before damning a lady of her station, likewise love little because they are forgiven little. No wonder publicans and sinners so often press into the Kingdom ahead of those whose vaunted respectability is a cloak for their arrogant self-righteousness.

II. THE PARABLE OF THE UNFORGIVING DEBTOR OR THE UNMERCIFUL SERVANT

"Therefore is the kingdom of heaven likened unto a certain king, who would make a reckoning with his servants. And when he had begun to reckon, one was brought unto him, that owed him ten thousand talents. But forasmuch as he had not wherewith to pay, his lord commanded him to be sold, and his wife, and children, and all that he had, and payment to be made. The servant therefore fell down and worshipped him, saying, Lord, have patience with me, and I will pay thee all. And the lord of that servant, being moved with compassion, released him, and forgave him the debt. But that servant went out, and found one of his fellow-servants, who owed him a hundred shillings: and he laid hold on him, and took him by the throat, saying, Pay what thou owest. So his fellow-servant fell down and besought him, saying, Have patience with me, and I will pay thee. And he would not: but went and cast him into prison, till he should pay that which was due. So when his fellow-servants saw what was done, they were exceeding sorry, and came and told unto their lord all that was done. Then his lord called him unto him, and saith to him, Thou wicked servant, I forgave thee all that debt, because thou besoughtest me: shouldest not thou also have had mercy on thy fellow-servant, even as I had mercy on thee? And his lord was wroth, and delivered him to the tormentors, till he should pay all that was due. So shall also my heavenly Father do unto you, if ye forgive not every one his brother from your hearts."

St. Matthew 18 : 23–35.

II

CHRIST'S disciples often quarrelled about their personal prominence in His forthcoming Kingdom. It may have been their rivalries, or St. Peter's private difficulties which prompted his inquiry about how many times he should forgive an offending brother. The Apostle tentatively suggested the answer to his question by adding another—"Until seven times?" Disregarding this broad hint, Jesus astonished His impulsive but lovable follower by the emphatic declaration: "I say not unto thee, Until seven times; *Until seventy times seven*"!—that is, without stint. The drama in two acts which follows amplifies His mandate. It is a first class example of the Oriental language which rarely lost itself in the wilderness of sentimentality, and led its audiences to refreshing oases of realism depicted in pungent phrases.

The first scene opens in the court of an Eastern monarch exercising despotic power over the persons and the property of his subjects. He commands his ministers of state, who are intrusted with large funds, to account for their disbursement. Before the king had well begun his examination, he discovered that an

official of the royal treasury was on the wrong side of
the ledger to the enormous amount of twelve million
dollars in American currency. The rascal must have
embezzled the annual taxes of the whole country.
Confronted by his conscienceless theft, he whined and
grovelled at the feet of his lord, begging for time and
he would restore every penny. Needless to say, he
promised the impossible. But the king, being a mag-
nanimous man, was so melted by his minister's hu-
miliation that he wiped out the debt and freely forgave the debtor. The next act in the drama reverses
the situation. It shows us how the grand vizier who
had so recently escaped his just deserts as a debtor
behaved as a creditor. One of his household slaves
owed him the paltry sum of less than twenty dollars.
The poor wretch offered the identical plea his default-
ing master had made to his sovereign: "Have patience
with me, and I will pay thee." Surely the forgiven
servant, remembering the amazing clemency he had
obtained, will promptly forgive the debt. But no:
he seizes the suppliant by the throat and hurls him into
prison. There he might have remained till death released him had not his case come to the ears of the
king. Upon receiving the information, he summoned
the unmerciful servant, committed him to the tor-
turers who placed him on the rack, and sentenced him

to close confinement until his gigantic obligation should be paid in full. Here the curtain falls on the sordid official. Betrayed by his perfidy and greed, he perished miserably.

These extraordinary scenes are intended to enforce the edict of forgiveness. Jesus was well aware that no law of the Kingdom is more difficult for man to obey. The patient pardon of wrongs done against one's self is constantly resisted by the lust for revenge and retaliation deeply entrenched in the individual and also in society. Yet these passions have to be subdued before the mutual confidence and good will which are Heaven's cement for earth's divisions can become available. Hence the telling contrasts of this parable. The monarch's generosity is typical of God's loving kindness; the unmerciful servant's conduct is a terrible contradiction of the clemency he had received. His doom shows that until men and nations are willing to forgive each other's offenses, God cannot pardon them. The gracious consideration He manifests in Christ is the source and inspiration of our charity and long suffering. In this spirit Jesus lived and died. The prayer He offered for those who nailed Him to the Holy Rood: "Father, forgive them, they know not what they do," is the divinest flower of His blameless life. Isabella's eloquent plea for the life of her brother

in "Measure for Measure" is perhaps the finest com-
ment upon the parable in dramatic literature.

> "Alas, alas!
> Why, all the souls that were were forfeit once;
> And He that might the vantage best have took
> Found out the remedy.   How would you be,
> If He, which is the top of judgment, should
> But judge you as you are?   O, think on that;
> And mercy then will breathe within your lips,
> Like man new made."

III. THE PARABLE OF EQUAL PAY FOR UNEQUAL WORK

"But many shall be last that are first; and first that are last. For the kingdom of heaven is like unto a man that was a householder, who went out early in the morning to hire laborers into his vineyard. And when he had agreed with the laborers for a shilling a day, he sent them into his vineyard. And he went out about the third hour, and saw others standing in the marketplace idle; and to them he said, Go ye also into the vineyard, and whatsoever is right I will give you. And they went their way. Again he went out about the sixth and the ninth hour, and did likewise. And about the eleventh hour he went out, and found others standing; and he saith unto them, Why stand ye here all the day idle? They say unto him, Because no man hath hired us. He saith unto them, Go ye also into the vineyard. And when even was come, the lord of the vineyard saith unto his steward, Call the laborers, and pay them their hire, beginning from the last unto the first. And when they came that were hired about the eleventh hour, they received every man a shilling. And when the first came, they supposed that they would receive more; and they likewise received every man a shilling. And when they received it, they murmured against the householder, saying, These last have spent but one hour, and thou hast made them equal unto us, who have borne the burden of the day and the scorching heat. But he answered and said to one of them, Friend, I do thee no wrong: didst not thou agree with me for a shilling? Take up that which is thine, and go thy way; it is my will to give unto this last, even as unto thee. Is it not lawful for me to do what I will with mine own? or is thine eye evil, because I am good? So the last shall be first, and the first last."

St. Matthew 19 : 30; 20 : 1–16.

The Child

"Whosoever shall receive this child in my name receiveth me: and whosoever shall receive me receiveth him that sent me: for he that is least among you all, the same shall be great."—Luke 9 : 48.

The Leaven

The Hidden Treasure

The Net

The Secret Growth of the Seed

The Prodigal Son

The Barren Fig Tree

The Good Samaritan

III

THIS story is prefaced by the incident of the rich young man whose strong sense of material possessions overcame his faith. When Jesus told him to surrender his wealth for the relief of the poor, his worldly prudence vanquished his pious resolution and he sorrowfully declined the exacting overture. As the Master watched him depart, He observed, with even greater sorrow: "It is easier for a camel to go through a needle's eye, than for a rich man to enter into the kingdom of God."[1] Whereupon St. Peter voiced the mind of his fellow disciples in asking what their reward would be for the sacrifices they had made. Although the question savored of presumption tinctured with ambition, Jesus promptly assured them that those who shared the Kingdom's perils should be its future lawgivers and judges. But He checked the complacency of these immature followers by His announcement that "many shall be last that are first, and first that are last." This principle is illuminated by the story of a man who owned one of the many vineyards of Judæa. He farmed his land, engaged the laborers, paid their wages

[1] St. Matthew 19 : 24.

65

and pocketed the profits. Sorely needing extra help, he hastened to the market place where it could usually be found no less than five times in one day: at six and nine in the morning, at high noon, and at three and five in the afternoon. On each visit he secured workmen for his vineyard. But when the first group, who had toiled from sunrise to sunset, found that the later groups received the same wages that were given to those who had borne the heat and burden of the day, they entered what seemed to be a reasonable protest. The master heard them patiently, but did not change his decision. He reminded the complainants that they had been equitably treated, and that if he chose to pay an equal wage for unequal service, this was his own affair. He might have added that the short time laborers, like so many of their kind today, were idle from necessity, not from choice. They tarried in some instances until the eleventh hour, because no man had hired them.

This parable conjoins with that of "The Prodigal Son" to magnify the riches of God's grace toward all who accept the Gospel's invitation, even though they enter His vineyard when life's sands are rapidly running out. For in the realm of His eternal life there is neither more nor less; early nor late; all its recipients are the sheep of one flock and one shepherd. St. Paul's fundamental argument that the just shall live by faith, not works, derives its authority from the story before us. It proclaims the universality of salvation, and encourages such as are disposed to cry: "Too late!" to enter the Kingdom here and now. But the parable does not warrant the idea that tardy comers into God's Kingdom appropriate its blessings as readily as those who come early. Spiritual development is not insured by "absent treatment" any more than intellectual culture is attained by sleeping in a library. No Christian can pass at a bound from religious pupilage to religious authority. Yet it should be noted that individuals and nations coming late into the Kingdom have in some historic instances outdistanced those among whom the Faith originated. Citizenship in God's Commonwealth may be forfeited by the "evil eye" (verse 15), which looks upon less favored peoples with suspicion and contempt. The scepter of Christian civilization may be retransferred from the West to the East unless we sedulously maintain sympathetic understanding and sacrificial service toward the whole world as the object of Christ's Redemption.

IV. THE PARABLE OF THE LOST SHEEP

"Now all the publicans and sinners were drawing near unto him to hear him. And both the Pharisees and the scribes murmured, saying, This man receiveth sinners, and eateth with them.

"And he spake unto them this parable, saying, What man of you, having a hundred sheep, and having lost one of them, doth not leave the ninety and nine in the wilderness, and go after that which is lost, until he find it? And when he hath found it, he layeth it on his shoulders, rejoicing. And when he cometh home, he calleth together his friends and his neighbors, saying unto them, Rejoice with me, for I have found my sheep which was lost. I say unto you, that even so there shall be joy in heaven over one sinner that repenteth, more than over ninety and nine righteous persons, who need no repentance."

St. Luke 15 : 1–7.

IV

CONCEIVE for yourselves the circumstances surrounding this and the two succeeding parables. The publicans and sinners who heard them were drawn by the Master's exposure of their overlords and His benevolent bearing toward themselves. They were also conversant with the material He so deftly wove into these three stories specially addressed to the lost sheep of the House of Israel. But He gave a new significance to the word "*lost.*" For a sheep is *lost* when it wanders aimlessly from the flock; a coin is *lost* when it ceases to circulate for commercial purposes; a son is *lost* when he squanders his God-given faculties in self-destroying sinful pursuits. The elder brother, too, is *lost* because he cherishes ill will and rancor toward the newly returned prodigal.

The plain tale of "The Lost Sheep" embodies the Master's mind in a picturesque and pathetic manner which poets, artists and musicians have embellished. Since a large part of Palestine's property consisted of flocks of sheep, their protection was an imperative duty rendered hazardous by prowling wolves, armed robbers and the sheep's tendency to wander. If but

one was missing the village shepherd at once left the
ninety and nine in the fold, sought until he found the
stray sheep, and brought it home again amid his neighbors' congratulations. These felicitous pastoral imageries adorn the pivotal truth of God's solicitude for
each single individual soul's welfare. Christ's detes-
tation of all artificial social barriers reflected the
Father's heart. His passion for the inward and outward freedom of every human personality is the source
of modern democracy and fraternity. St. Paul's
avowal that in his Lord "there cannot be Greek and
Jew, circumcision and uncircumcision, barbarian, Scy-
thian, bondman, freeman; but Christ is all, and in
all,"[1] is the grand charter of humanity's ultimate
unity and brotherhood. Notwithstanding the resistance of separatists and their allies, the universalism
of the Old Testament prophets and the New Testament apostles slowly permeates our provincial narrow-
ness.

The parable also admonishes us concerning the
fatal proclivity to wander. Purposeless living is re-
sponsible for about one half the world's undoing. Men
have not to actively cultivate wickedness. It is fully
served when they aimlessly float with the current till
it sweeps them into the dangerous rapids from which

[1] Colossians 3 : 11.

escape is difficult. The majority of reprobates begin by sauntering in forbidden paths like silly sheep. It is also a great comfort to learn from this narrative that God seeks those who are lost in the bleak wilderness of a blighted life far more eagerly than they seek Him. Francis Thompson describes that search in his inspired poem, "The Hound of Heaven." With merciful persistence and unperturbed pace he tracks down the foolish and the desolate. Their ability to escape their own welfare cannot outwit the Father's determination to rescue them from themselves.

V. THE PARABLE OF THE LOST COIN

"Or what woman having ten pieces of silver, if she lose one piece, doth not light a lamp, and sweep the house, and seek diligently until she find it? And when she hath found it, she calleth together her friends and neighbors, saying, Rejoice with me, for I have found the piece which I had lost. Even so, I say unto you, there is joy in the presence of the angels of God over one sinner that repenteth."

St. Luke 15 : 8–10.

V

THE parable of "The Lost Coin" is not a mere replica of that of "The Lost Sheep." On the contrary, it was given for the special benefit of the un-privileged women who keenly appreciated this domestic incident which St. Luke records in his Evangel of penitence, restoration and thanksgiving. Besides, the sheep was lost *outside* the fold, whereas the coin was lost *inside* the house. The point is that these despised outcasts to whom the Master ministered were as surely Abraham's children as the haughtiest Pharisee in the land. The housewife's scrupulous search for her coin symbolized God's determination to gather to Himself all who had been arbitrarily shut out by their domineering superiors.

It was common then, as it is now, for some hardworking woman, who had to practice the strictest economy to make ends meet, to lose a single coin which nevertheless meant much to her and her family. Knowing she must find it if the household was not to be deprived of its actual necessities, she ransacked every room in the house till the coin was recovered. Simple enough, is it not? and nothing more than a matter for the women's friendly gossip at the village well. Yet so near is God's grandeur to the lowliest human lot, that Jesus makes the incident a symbol of celestial happiness, and declares "there is joy in the presence of the angels of God over one sinner that repenteth."[1] The entire narrative harmonizes with Christ's controlling idea of the Father who will not be satisfied until all His lost ones, lone and sad, are made partakers of His Divine nature.

[1] St. Luke 15 : 10.

VI. THE PARABLE OF THE LOST SON

"And he said, A certain man had two sons: and the younger of them said to his father, Father, give me the portion of thy substance that falleth to me. And he divided unto them his living. And not many days after, the younger son gathered all together and took his journey into a far country; and there he wasted his substance with riotous living. And when he had spent all, there arose a mighty famine in that country; and he began to be in want. And he went and joined himself to one of the citizens of that country; and he sent him into his fields to feed swine. And he would fain have filled his belly with the husks that the swine did eat: and no man gave unto him. But when he came to himself he said, How many hired servants of my father's have bread enough and to spare, and I perish here with hunger! I will arise and go to my father, and will say unto him, Father, I have sinned against heaven, and in thy sight: I am no more worthy to be called thy son: make me as one of thy hired servants. And he arose, and came to his father. But while he was yet afar off, his father saw him, and was moved with compassion, and ran, and fell on his neck, and kissed him. And the son said unto him, Father, I have sinned against heaven, and in thy sight: I am no more worthy to be called thy son. But the father said to his servants, Bring forth quickly the best robe, and put it on him; and put a ring on his hand, and shoes on his feet: and bring the fatted calf, and kill it, and let us eat, and make merry: for this my son was dead, and is alive again; he was lost, and is found. And they began to be merry. Now his elder son was in the field: and as he came and drew nigh to the house, he heard music and dancing. And he called to him one of the servants, and inquired what these things might be. And he said unto him, Thy brother is come; and thy father hath killed the fatted calf, because he hath received him safe and sound. But he was angry, and would not go in: and his father came out, and entreated him. But he answered and said to his father, Lo, these many years do I serve thee, and I never transgressed a commandment of thine; and yet thou never gavest me a kid, that I might make merry with my friends: but when this thy son came, who hath devoured thy living with harlots, thou killedst for him the fatted calf. And he said unto him, Son, thou art ever with me, and all that is mine is thine. But it was meet to make merry and be glad: for this thy brother was dead, and is alive again; and was lost, and is found."

St. Luke 15 : 11–32.

VI

CRABB ROBINSON, the early Victorian diarist and sceptic, exclaimed as he looked for the first time on Raphael's "Sistine Madonna" in the Dresden Gallery: "Now I believe in the Incarnation!" Yet the Master's story of "The Lost Son" far exceeds in transcendent grace and loveliness that marvellous picture of the Virgin and her Babe. Nothing in art or literature presents a more vital theme or one so symmetrical in its unity of theme and treatment. In truth, the very heart of God overflows in this parable. It leaves emotion in the soul and music in the memory of saints and sinners alike. Its portrait of the Everlasting Father makes every other delineation of His character either contributory or negligible. Yet Jesus did not paint that portrait in the colors of some remote, imponderable realm beyond the vicissitudes of time and place. It originated in His perfect fellowship with the Father, and He used the tragic incident of a headstrong prodigal to transmit it to mankind. Bent on escaping his rustic surroundings, and lured by the call of the wild, this young man bawled for his liberty in a senseless mood, grabbed his share of the family estate, and immediately set out for the "far country." There he threw off every sanction and restraint, and gave free rein to his animalism. He imagined he owned his wealth, whereas in reality his wealth captured and jailed him as securely as though he had been confined in a deep pit walled with glass. Excess is always morally stupid, even in its most seductive guise, and those who take to it usually fumble life's game and come to grief. Thus gulled by his money, and by the human vultures who preyed on him, he practiced without stint the worst vices until his brief delirium burned itself out. Then, driven to the wall, he was compelled to beg for the most ignominious job a Jew could conceive—the feeding of swine. Moreover, he "would fain have filled his belly with the husks that the swine did eat: and no man gave unto him" (verse 16). The blacklegs, cheats and harlots who had devoured his substance and his manhood deserted him in a body. Truly he was in "a far country": a land in which debauchery superseded decency, and where his soul wilted. There he languished, keenly aware that "a sorrow's crown of sorrow is remembering happier things," until his desperation and nakedness drove him home.

He determined to return to his father's house, though he died on its door step. I dare not attempt to describe his welcome. Why paint the lily white or gild refined gold? But I own that I cannot read how the aged father *saw* his ragged, sorefooted son while he was still a long way down the dusty road, and *ran* to meet him, without being deeply moved. Think of the selfless love that gave such sight to those fading eyes, and such speed to those tired limbs! Then reflect that this is the one authorized portrait of the God we adore: as He was, and is, and shall be forever.

The elder brother has been exploited at some length in the interpretation of the parable. To be sure, his complaints and denunciations were not entirely groundless. Yet he stands for those outwardly correct people who are immoral at the core: nothing better than "sounding brass and tinkling cymbal," because they lack that charity which is the height of good, the hate of ill, truth's triumph and falsehood's overthrow. But why linger with this irreconcilable man? Let us rather give heed to the father's explanation: "it was meet to make merry and be glad: for this thy brother was dead, and is alive again; and was lost, and is found" (verse 32). The celebration of the prodigal's return bespeaks infinite possibilities for good in the worst of us. Its joyous mirth reminds some churlish and sulky "elder brethren" that since God never ceases to love those He loses, He can never lose those He thus loves.

CHAPTER IV
PARABLES OF MORAL INSTRUCTION AND WARNING

I. THE PARABLE OF THE TWO BUILDERS AND THEIR HOUSES

"Every one therefore that heareth these words of mine, and doeth them, shall be likened unto a wise man, who built his house upon the rock; and the rain descended, and the floods came, and the winds blew, and beat upon that house; and it fell not: for it was founded upon the rock. And every one that heareth these words of mine, and doeth them not, shall be likened unto a foolish man, who built his house upon the sand: and the rain descended, and the floods came, and the winds blew, and smote upon that house, and it fell: and great was the fall thereof."

St. Matthew 7 : 24–27.

See also St. Luke 6 : 47–49.

Chapter IV

PARABLES OF MORAL INSTRUCTION AND WARNING

I

JESUS did not confine His working days to the carpenter's shop at Nazareth; He visited the surrounding villages and towns to aid in constructing their houses and shops. It was therefore natural that He should compare the building of character with the building of a house. St. Matthew and St. Luke place this parable at the close of that great blue print of God's House of Life—"The Sermon on the Mount"— with which Christ began his Galilean ministry. Several essentials are suggested for life's lasting structure: the first being a competent architect. The Master's desire that all who heard Him should obey His teachings indicates that these contain God's purposes for man's being. His plan for life has symmetry, durability and beauty. Its commanding prospect is flooded with the warm light of that love which honors all men. Its windows look out on those diversified scenes of happiness and woe which evoke the inmate's sympathetic

83

understanding. The doors of its outer chamber are open to the defenseless and the disconsolate. Its inner sanctuary is consecrated to that fellowship which enables the resident spirit to say:

"Here, O my Lord! I see Thee face to face;
  Here would I touch and handle things unseen;
  Here grasp with firmer hand eternal grace,
  And all my weariness upon Thee lean."

The second essential is a solid foundation. The life founded on God's Fatherhood, man's Brotherhood, the imperishable value of every individual, and sacrificial service for others, is built upon the Rock of Ages. But to reach it we must dig down, penetrating below surface hearing of the word to its actual fulfilment "in deeds more strong than all poetic thought." The third essential is that this plan shall suit all periods, circumstances and conditions of humanity. Who doubts that if the laws of Christ for human life had universal observance as they have spiritual authority they would transform the world? The parable also intimates that every structure of the soul, whatever its foundation, is subjected to furious tempests of opposition, cold rains of adversity, and the inundation of bodily death. The house reared on the sands of cupidity and time-serving crumbles and falls. So fell the gigantic edifice of the Roman State, notwithstanding its imperial might. So fall daily, personalities and, ever and anon, even governments which in their outward aspects are stable enough. But the house founded on Christ's life and likeness weathers every storm, and is the stronger for its assaults. How much saner His plan is than that espoused in the specious thinking of a modern poetess:

"Safe upon the solid rock, the ugly houses stand,
    Come and see my shining palace built upon the sand."

The invitation belies the facts. The noblest, fairest lives, and the historic institutions endeared to us by their service to man, have been founded upon patient justice and enduring truth. Yet were they "ugly," sagacious people would still choose the leaden casket containing the treasure, and reject the golden casket concealing the death's head.[1]

[1] *The Merchant of Venice,* Act II, Scene VII.

II. THE PARABLE OF THE TWO SONS

"But what think ye? A man had two sons; and he came to the first, and said, Son, go work today in the vineyard. And he answered and said, I will not: but afterward he repented himself, and went. And he came to the second, and said likewise. And he answered, and said, I go, sir: and went not. Which of the two did the will of his father? They say, The first. Jesus saith unto them, Verily I say unto you, that the publicans and the harlots go into the kingdom of God before you. For John came unto you in the way of righteousness, and ye believed him not; but the publicans and the harlots believed him: and ye, when ye saw it, did not even repent yourselves afterward, that ye might believe him."

St. Matthew 21 : 28–32.

II

Formalists who paraded their self-consequence, offered long prayers at the street corners and gave their alms ostentatiously, got a short shrift from Jesus. His sharp contrasts in this parable pricked their pretensions. It is a first rate example of the destructive criticism their deceptive vagaries elicited from Him. The son who at first denied his father's request, but afterward repented and obeyed it, represents the publicans and sinners; while the second son who responded to his father's request, and then treacherously evaded it, represents the Scribes and Pharisees. Plainly the penitence which changed a man's intention was a sure passport to Christ's approval. He never condoned the extortions of the publicans or the orgies of the sinners, any more than He indorsed the corrupt morals and icy manners of the Scribes and Pharisees. But a transgressor's contrition was precious in His sight. If John the Baptist quickened the national conscience, Jesus threw open the gates of God's Kingdom to every believing soul sorry for its sin.

The parable also implies a warning against the dangers of emotionalism. Sentimentalists are prone to connect large resolves with small results. Reuben, that unstable son of Jacob, preferred the shepherd's piping by the stream to the trumpet blasts summoning him to battle. "I will lay down my life for Thee!" cried St. Peter. Yet when he should have been at his Master's side he was warming himself at the fire, and denying Him to an inquisitive servant maid. Intense feelings which are a spur to decisive action are commendable, but they are hurtful when used as a substitute for action. Again, the waste of life's opportunities is man's rank treason; whereas the faintest effort to fulfil them diverts life's stream of tendency in the right direction. It distressed Jesus that men whose ancestral prophets and heroes had bequeathed them the loftiest ideals and examples, should notwithstanding play the fool and the knave, but He rejoiced to see the spiritually destitute and despairing set out for the City of God.

The capital offense of the religious man is pride and self-sufficiency, even more so than impurity and sloth; yet the Scribes and Pharisees were so enamoured with themselves that they could not detect this source of their moral impotence. The Master's glad tidings were their abhorrence. They were always "going," but they never "went," whereas the nondescripts they flouted promised nothing and did a great deal. Phylacteries, rituals and ceremonies have their place. But when they become merely outward decorations for inward disloyalty they are obnoxious to God and man. It is all too easy to adore a wooden Christ on a wooden cross while the real Christ of love and justice is being recrucified. What we need is the Cross planted in the heart of every Christian and in the soul of the Church. In the words of John Drinkwater,

> "We know the paths wherein our feet should press;
>   Across our hearts are written Thy decrees;
> Yet now, O Lord, be merciful to bless
>   With more than these.
>
> "Grant us the will to fashion as we feel,
>   Grant us the strength to labor as we know,
> Grant us the purpose, ribb'd and edged with steel,
>   To strike the blow.
>
> "Knowledge we ask not—knowledge Thou hast lent;
>   But, Lord, the will—there lies our bitter need;
> Give us to build above the deep intent
>   The deed, the deed."

III. THE PARABLE OF THE CHILDREN PLAYING IN THE MARKET PLACES

"Whereunto then shall I liken the men of this generation, and to what are they like? They are like unto children that sit in the market-place, and call one to another; who say, We piped unto you, and ye did not dance; we wailed, and ye did not weep. For John the Baptist is come eating no bread nor drinking wine; and ye say, He hath a demon. The Son of man is come eating and drinking; and ye say, Behold, a gluttonous man, and a winebibber, a friend of publicans and sinners! And wisdom is justified of all her children."

St. Luke 7 : 31–35.

III

THIS scene of children at play furnishes a bright
gleam of innocent happiness, aglow with the promise
of life's morning, unshadowed by its later cares and
griefs. The memories of Christ's childhood at Nazareth
may have suggested His comparisons. For there His
glorious Mother always permitted Him to be Himself.
His full orbed manhood was not disfigured by the scars
which harsh parental discipline has left on the souls
of many sensitive and gifted men and women. When
He placed His strong arms around the frail bodies of
these Galilean youngsters, and drew them to His
heart, He reacted to the beautiful training of His
own childhood. The first group of little ones mentioned here was eager to play games imitating wedding
feasts and their associations of music and merriment.
Then the children's mercurial moods changed to solemn
funerals, attended by wailing mourners, who beat
their breasts and chanted doleful tributes to the dead.
But some petty quarrel had left the second group un-
friendly and capricious. They drew away from their
playmates and mocked their invitation to join in the
games. The winsomeness of the parable is to the manner born. Its naturalness can be verified on any
playground. Some of its earliest interpreters applied

the story to the difference between the personalities
of Jesus and John the Baptist. Later ones hold that
it illustrates the blind vengeance wreaked upon many
of the world's greatest benefactors who were regarded
askance as dangerous zealots and agitators to be sup-
pressed, or even killed. So was it with the tender
Jesus and His austere Forerunner. They came into
the stuffy, enervating atmosphere of their period like
a fresh breeze from the sea or the melody of children's
voices in a lonely home. But neither John's asceticism
nor Christ's social tendencies pleased the rulers of the
land. They stood aloof and refused to acquiesce with
John's vigil in the Jordan Valley, or with Jesus as He
freely mingled with men, women and children. As
they saw them, the one was a fanatic; the other a
seditionist and an outlaw.

But "wisdom is justified of all her children." They
may don the monastic habit of Savonarola, or like St.
Francis, become "God's troubadours" to joyously
transform the soul of a callous age. These different
methods subserve the same cause and speed the Kingdom's progress. Both Jesus and John moved heaven-
ward in the light of God, and vindicated His Wisdom.
But the leaders of their generation, hide bound and
jealous, skulked in the dark byways of prejudice and
unbelief.

IV. THE PARABLE OF THE WICKED VINEDRESSERS

"Hear another parable: There was a man that was a householder, who planted a vineyard, and set a hedge about it, and digged a winepress in it, and built a tower, and let it out to husbandmen, and went into another country. And when the season of the fruits drew near, he sent his servants to the husbandmen, to receive his fruits. And the husbandmen took his servants, and beat one, and killed another, and stoned another. Again, he sent other servants more than the first; and they did unto them in like manner. But afterward he sent unto them his son, saying, They will reverence my son. But the husbandmen, when they saw the son, said among themselves, This is the heir; come, let us kill him, and take his inheritance. And they took him, and cast him forth out of the vineyard, and killed him. When therefore the lord of the vineyard shall come, what will he do unto those husbandmen? They say unto him, He will miserably destroy those miserable men, and will let out the vineyard unto other husbandmen, who shall render him the fruits in their seasons."

St. Matthew 21 : 33–41.

IV

DESPITE its renowned humor, Cervantes' immortal romance, "Don Quixote," is one of the saddest things in literature: a book which tells of a chivalrous contestant for the grace, the courage and high enterprise of a day forever gone. This parable also discloses what seems to be a far greater misadventure: nothing less than the Master's anticipation of His death. He came to His own, and His own received Him not. When He appeared, the Israel which Isaiah compared to a vineyard on a sunny hillside, planted with the choicest vines, had become barren and desolate. The first fruits of her increase, which Jeremiah asserted was holiness unto the Lord, had vanished with the prophetic age. The people concerning whom St. Paul afterwards asserted that theirs was "the adoption, and the glory, and the covenants, and the giving of the law, and the service of God, and the promises,"[1] were the prey of internal antipathies and dissensions and foreign exactions. Jehovah's choice of Israel, however, was an election to world service; in which her responsibilities went hand in hand with her rights.

[1] Romans 9 : 4.

When so highly favored a nation no longer produced those politicians of God who urged it to fresh achievements for Him, its sterility in leadership presaged national ruin. Signs of this ruin were already upon Israel when Christ made His great remonstrance against her further betrayal of the mission assigned her. Had not Amos been hunted out of Bethel because of his social message; Jeremiah driven into exile for the sake of his illustrious covenant of the spirit; Ezekiel treated as though he were a buffoon by his fellow exiles in Babylon? Jesus, remembering these harryings and persecutions, decreed His own doom in the cry: "A prophet cannot perish out of Jerusalem!" Obscurantists to a man, unreservedly committed to the dictates of their class, and hating all reforms with a fervor equalled only by their stubborness, His antagonists deserved this indictment. They built the sepulchres of God's heroes, garnished the tombs of the righteous, and said: "If we had been living in the days of our fathers, we would not have joined them in shedding the blood of the prophets." Whereupon Christ answered: "So you are witnesses against yourselves, that you are sons of those who killed the prophets!"[1]

His relentless arraignment is emphasized by the story of a band of desperadoes who seized the oppor-

[1] St. Matthew 23 : 30-31 (Moffatt's Translation).

tunity offered by their kindly master's absence to
beat and slay his unoffending agents. They were no
longer reasoning beings, but creatures resembling
beasts of prey, who completed their infamy by as-
sassinating his own son. The parable records and
justice approves the retribution that followed their
insane wickedness. Yet we should remember that
Israel has not been the sole offender, nor are the sins
of consuming personal interest and fanatical nation-
alism limited to her annals. Although this parable
was given for her warning nineteen centuries ago, it
did not prevent her catastrophe, nor has it prevented
the later downfall of even stronger nations. Its lesson,
solidified by their experience, and engraved on history
as with a pen of iron, is as germane for us as it was
for the ancient Jews. From such fearful perfidy and
its inevitable doom may the Lord deliver the richly
privileged peoples of the twentieth century!

V. THE PARABLE OF THE MARRIAGE BANQUET

"And Jesus answered and spake again in parables unto them, saying, The kingdom of heaven is likened unto a certain king, who made a marriage feast for his son, and sent forth his servants to call them that were bidden to the marriage feast: and they would not come. Again he sent forth other servants, saying, Tell them that are bidden, Behold, I have made ready my dinner; my oxen and my fatlings are killed, and all things are ready: come to the marriage feast. But they made light of it, and went their ways, one to his own farm, another to his merchandise; and the rest laid hold on his servants, and treated them shamefully, and killed them. But the king was wroth; and he sent his armies, and destroyed those murderers, and burned their city. Then saith he to his servants, The wedding is ready, but they that were bidden were not worthy. Go ye therefore unto the partings of the highways, and as many as ye shall find, bid to the marriage feast. And those servants went out into the highways, and gathered together all as many as they found, both bad and good: and the wedding was filled with guests."

St. Matthew 22 : 1–10.

See also St. Luke 14 : 16–24.

V

St. Matthew states that this feast was a royal banquet, but St. Luke depicts it more simply as a supper spread by a private individual for his friends. The first Evangelist also points out that the monarch's invitation was repeated, and that those to whom it was given abused and even murdered the royal messengers. St. Luke does not mention this feature, but he relates at some length the excuses of the guests who were first invited.

Again, St. Matthew linked the parable in question with that of the wicked husbandmen, thus showing that its main purpose was to exhibit the obduracy of those recalcitrants who turned a deaf ear to God's repeated appeals through Jesus, that they should enjoy that fellowship with Him which ushered in the hour of spiritual feasting and of song. St. Luke does not exclude this meaning, but according to his wont, he exalts the universalism of the Kingdom, and describes in detail the three groups of invited guests. The first and largest group consists of the typical respectable Jew of the time, proud of his race and religion, but preoccupied by his business or domestic affairs.

The second group consists of "the poor and maimed and blind and lame": shabby and down at the heel; frequenters of the slums and lanes, for whom life was a constant struggle. The third group consists of humanity's floatsam and jetsam who drift in the backwaters of society, and are often stigmatized as its scum.

Both parables, as finished examples of creative art, are capable of more than one interpretation. Some expositors dwell on their presentation of the Gospel's abundant provisions; others on the extension of the invitation to partake of them to every class and condition. Not one need be left outside, for Jesus welcomes all mankind. The comparison with a royal marriage suggests the unifying force and bliss of Christian communion. Those who pled their various engagements were unaware that Christ's religion covers every avenue of human life and work. "Raise the stone, and there thou shalt find me. Cleave the wood and there am I," is a saying attributed to the Lord of the Gospel Feast. Francis Thompson visualized Him in noisy, bustling London. For that great poet, the city's traffic at Charing Cross was another Jacob's ladder reared between earth and heaven. Jesus still walked on the waters of the Thames, with its craft from many ports, as He had once walked on Galilee's

Lake. Such princes of religious imagination convince us that the omnipresent Christ offers the Kingdom's hospitality at all times and in all places, and by so doing shames the indifference and neglect of His invited guests.

VI. THE PARABLE OF THE UNFRUITFUL FIG TREE

"And he spake this parable; A certain man had a fig tree planted in his vineyard; and he came seeking fruit thereon, and found none. And he said unto the vinedresser, Behold, these three years I come seeking fruit on this fig tree, and find none: cut it down; why doth it also cumber the ground? And he answering saith unto him, Lord, let it alone this year also, till I shall dig about it, and dung it: and if it bear fruit thenceforth, well; but if not, thou shalt cut it down."

St. Luke 13 : 6–9.

VI

THE significance of "The Unfruitful Fig Tree" is intensified by the joy of Jesus in life itself and in life's fulfilment of its varied ends. The birds must build their nests, the meadows be clothed with grass, the clouds shed their rain upon the expectant soil, the sun pour warmth and radiance upon the earth. Any falling short in Nature disappointed Him. He also lamented the household lamp being thrust under the bed or covered over with a bushel. What was a lamp for, if not to be replenished, lit, and placed on a stand to give light to all in the home? Fishermen's nets and baskets were woven to be filled with fish. "Launch out into the deep!" was His command to those who complained: "We have caught nothing, though we toiled all night." He condemned the shiftlessness which breeds passivity and uselessness. For Him lassitude was an approach to actual turpitude. St. Paul reiterated these teachings in his exhortation: "in diligence not slothful; fervent in spirit; serving the lord."[1] Riches, genius, power—from the secular view-

[1] Romans 12 : 11.

103

point these are desirable objectives, demanding strenu-
ous effort. Yet riches are insatiable, genius is seldom
content, and power is ever on the wing. But conscious
growth in goodness is life's greatest, most joyous purpose and its subsequent perfection. Its satisfaction is
not found in camping by the wayside, but on the march
and in the thick of the fray.

Isaiah, in his well-known parable of the vineyard,
deplores its unfruitfulness except in wild grapes.
Jeremiah was similarly afflicted because the vine grown
from a promising seed turned out a degenerate plant.
Jesus, who had often read their flaming words of Re-
buke and Exhortation, thoroughly understood the perils
overhanging the nation symbolized by "The Barren
Fig Tree." It had not yet become a degenerate plant,
but it was aggravatingly slow; promising much, yielding nothing. As a picturesque presentation, the parable
bore directly upon those around Him who deliberately
thwarted Heaven's gifts and defeated their intention.
Spiritual energies which, like sap in the tree, should
bring forth the fruits of righteous living, while at the
same time developing the permanent qualities of character, were either unused or applied to ignoble pursuits.

The parable also stresses God's forbearance. The
tree in question cumbered the ground, and should

have been cut down to make room for a better specimen.   But it is given another chance and further
nourishment.   So is it with men and women.   The unrighteous need not remain unrighteous, nor the filthy
continue to wallow in their filth.   Hardened sinners
can be restored to health of soul and purity of life.
But they must coöperate with every step taken for
their relief.   Sir James M. Barrie, in his whimsical
play, "Dear Brutus," introduces several characters,
who stoutly contend that if their circumstances were
only different, they would become completely different
men and women.   When their circumstances suddenly
change for the better, however, the philanderer still
persists in his dirty tricks, the vain woman is still
discontented, the avaricious man still cheats,   "The
fault, dear Brutus," owns one of them, "is not in our
stars, but in ourselves."   In Barrie's play there may be
another chance for the minority who summon resolution
and break their chain.   But Christ's parable fills the
hopeless with hope.   It impregnates the dead in tres-
passes and sins with vital ideals.   It enables swamped
and useless lives to become as trees planted by rivers of
water, which bring forth their fruit in season.   Yet one
cannot avoid the conclusion that although grace and
mercy characterize this parable, judgment prepon-
derates in it.   The gardener's plea that the fig tree be

given one more year shows that our opportunities for repentance and betterment are strictly conditioned, and that the penalty for making sport of the Kingdom's beneficence is final exclusion from it.

CHAPTER V
PARABLES OF MORAL INSTRUCTION
AND WARNING
(CONTINUED)

I. THE PARABLE OF THE THREE TRAVELLERS OR THE COMPASSIONATE SAMARITAN

"And behold a certain lawyer stood up and made trial of him, saying, Teacher, what shall I do to inherit eternal life? And he said unto him, What is written in the law? how readest thou? And he answering said, Thou shat love the Lord thy God with all thy heart, and with all thy soul, and with all thy strength, and with all thy mind; and thy neighbor as thyself. And he said unto him, Thou hast answered right: this do, and thou shalt live. But he, desiring to justify himself, said unto Jesus, And who is my neighbor? Jesus made answer and said, A certain man was going down from Jerusalem to Jericho, and he fell among robbers, who both stripped him and beat him, and departed, leaving him half dead. And by chance a certain priest was going down that way: and when he saw him, he passed by on the other side. And in like manner a Levite also, when he came to the place, and saw him, passed by on the other side. But a certain Samaritan, as he journeyed, came where he was: and when he saw him, he was moved with compassion, and came to him, and bound up his wounds, pouring on them oil

109

and wine; and he set him on his own beast, and brought him to an inn, and took care of him. And on the morrow he took out two shillings, and gave them to the host, and said, Take care of him; and whatsoever thou spendest more, I, when I come back again, will repay thee. Which of these three, thinkest thou, proved neighbor unto him that fell among the robbers? And he said, He that showed mercy on him. And Jesus said unto him, Go, and do thou likewise."

St. Luke 10 : 25–37.

Chapter V

PARABLES OF MORAL INSTRUCTION AND
WARNING (*Continued*)

I

THE greatest art in any form instructs, not by moralizing, but by suggestion. It engages the imagination, which in turn commandeers the mind, and evokes its creative thinking. The parable before us is an instance of this process. No narrative has done so much to create in a shamefully selfish world the sense of personal responsibility for social redemption. Its influence in the organizing of numberless philanthropic agencies is an unanswerable reply to the first murderer's unfeeling query: "Am I my brother's keeper?" The lawyer in the picture who wished to vindicate himself by asking: "Who is neighbor to me?" was the prototype of those who still impose geographical boundaries on love's universal sway. In His reply, Jesus shows that that man is our neighbor who is in utmost need, though at the farthest Pole.

Sad to relate, each allusion in this story has been fettered by expositors who allegorized the whole in-

cident.   Jerusalem was Paradise, Jericho was the
present world, the traveler was Adam, the robbers
were hostile demons, the Priest was the Mosaic Law,
the Levite was the prophets, the Samaritan repre-
sented Jesus, the wounds of the unhappy victim were
disobedience, the beast was Christ's body, the two
pence, or "denarii," were the Father and the Son, the
inn was the Church.   Thus this entrancing story has
been marred by fantastic distortions, examples of
which could be multiplied indefinitely.   It is best to
leave them to a well-deserved obscurity, and keep the
purport of the parable steadily before us.

The lawyer's first question: "Master, what shall
I do to inherit eternal life?" elicited from Jesus the
three great laws binding on all supplicants for that
celestial estate: *love of God*, embracing mind, soul and
strength, as the sole end of a man's perfected being;
love of self, as the reverence due to God's sacred gift
in personality; *love of the neighbor*, the meaning of which
is elucidated in the incident that follows.   Then, and
too often now, the word neighbor signified for the majority those of their own blood, nation, tastes, habits
and conformity to custom.

Undoubtedly Jesus drew His own portrait in the
compassionate Samaritan.   For He, too, was a constant traveler, who made light of His own sufferings

that He might lighten the sufferings of others. But
what of the Priest and the Levite? They were pledged
by their holy vocation to aid their helpless country-
man in the ditch. Besides, they did not seek his
misery; it sought them, and made its piteous appeal to
their ordinary human instincts; not to mention their
patriotic and religious sentiments. But these were so
fossilized beneath their official shell that the Priest
and the Levite "passed by on the other side." Such
festering lilies smell far worse than the foulest weeds.
Here were two clerics who imagined themselves nothing less than lilies of Heaven's growth, but their dis-
graceful conduct emits a bad odor. Then came that
human "weed," rank and rejected, the heretical
Samaritan, despised and hated by his Jewish kinsmen
as a traitor to his blood and his faith, with whom the
Jews had no dealings. Nevertheless, this heterodox
son of God leapt from his beast, placed the wounded
man on it, took full care of him, and made provision
for his rest and recovery. Comments upon so con-
vincing a personalization of the conditions to be fulfilled by those who would inherit eternal life are wholly
superfluous. What a havoc this parable makes of
lives inconsistent with what the lips profess; of meticu-
lous insistence on creedal beliefs and other hoary de-
fenses of the ungodly religious. They shrink beneath

its searching light. It will live forever because it is the expression of the purest and most disinterested affection for mankind, given in terms untrammelled by conventional beliefs or popular prejudices. Summed up in a word it tells us that "love conquers everything." Those who cannot pass by stricken humanity deprived of any of its God ordained rights are His children and heirs. Were the alignment they constitute drawn according to the facts, it would cause consternation in institutional Christianity.

II. THE PARABLE OF THE VACANT HOUSE

"The unclean spirit when he is gone out of the man, passeth through waterless places, seeking rest, and finding none, he saith, I will turn back unto my house whence I came out. And when he is come, he findeth it swept and garnished. Then goeth he, and taketh to him seven other spirits more evil than himself; and they enter in and dwell there: and the last state of that man becometh worse than the first."

St. Luke 11 : 24–26.

II

THE author of "The Sleeping Bard," a Welsh poem of antiquity, sings of the loathsome spirits of treachery and deceit endeavoring to gain an entrance under cover of night into a small hillside Church. As they come near to it, they find to their disgust that the sacred fane is ablaze with light. The lamps of fidelity and sincerity illuminate its interior, and the baffled demons are compelled to retreat. The parable before us gives us the antithesis of that poem. It reveals the dangers of the vacant mind, and uses the then universal belief in diabolism to enforce its meaning. An evil spirit driven from a man's life seeks other harborage in the waste places such specters were supposed to haunt. Finding no opening for his malignancies, he hastens back to the soul from which he had been expelled, and discovers with sinister delight that what he calls "*my house*" is still empty, "swept and garnished." It is as though his return had been expected. He at once invites seven other demons to take joint possession with him of that man's life, and they make his last state "worse than the first."

Of all the perversities infecting human nature few equal those which this man practiced to avoid facing the vital issues of his own soul.

117

He was neither altogether praiseworthy nor altogether despicable, but vacuous and negative; forever on the fence between the ape and the angel. Though having a skin-deep respectability, his heart lacked "the expulsive power of a new affection." He detests the outcast demon, but hesitates to welcome Christ's guardian presence. Absolute loyalty to the God of all good is impossible to him. He may not openly transgress as unrestrained sinners do, but his moral stupidity encourages many iniquitious causes. Because his duty is wanting in conviction, it is akin to slavery. Without central beliefs or stabilizing aims, so spineless a specimen is easily swayed by windy notions and sinful temptations. The worm of superstition creeps out from the grave of his buried faith. Christ's candid exposure of the appalling consequences which devastate the flabby soul is ratified by experience. He was not intent on increasing the company of His adherents by lowering the standards of discipleship. Nothing but righteousness would suffice, and nothing but *His* righteousness was sufficient to irradiate life's house with love, truth and justice. For when any soul becomes a palace to entertain the Christ and a fortress to defend Him, the worst of demons may assault, but they cannot capture it.

III. THE PARABLES OF THE TALENTS AND
THE POUNDS

"For it is as when a man, going into another country, called his own servants, and delivered unto them his goods. And unto one he gave five talents, to another two, to another one; to each according to his several ability; and he went on his journey. Straightway he that received the five talents went and traded with them, and made other five talents. In like manner he also that received the two gained other two. But he that received the one went away and digged in the earth, and hid his lord's money. Now after a long time the lord of those servants cometh, and maketh a reckoning with them. And he that received the five talents came and brought other five talents, saying, Lord, thou deliveredst unto me five talents: lo, I have gained other five talents. His lord said unto him, Well done, good and faithful servant: thou hast been faithful over a few things, I will set thee over many things; enter thou into the joy of thy lord. And he also that received the two talents came and said, Lord, thou deliveredst unto me two talents: lo, I have gained

119

other two talents. His lord said unto him, Well done, good and faithful servant: thou has been faithful over a few things, I will set thee over many things; enter thou into the joy of thy lord. And he also that received the one talent came and said, Lord, I knew thee that thou art a hard man, reaping where thou didst not sow, and gathering where thou didst not scatter; and I was afraid, and went away and hid thy talent in the earth: lo, thou hast thine own. But his lord answered and said unto him, Thou wicked and slothful servant, thou knewest that I reap where I sowed not, and gather where I did not scatter; thou oughtest therefore to have put my money to the bankers, and at my coming I should have received back mine own with interest. Take ye away therefore the talent from him, and give it unto him that hath the ten talents. For unto every one that hath shall be given, and he shall have abundance: but from him that hath not, even that which he hath shall be taken away. And cast ye out the unprofitable servant into the outer darkness: there shall be the weeping and the gnashing of teeth."

St. Matthew 25 : 14–30.

See also St. Luke 19 : 12–27.

III

CLEMENT of Alexandria attributed to Jesus the speech of the money market in the following saying: "Show yourselves true bankers, rejecting the counterfeit and holding fast the sterling." This utterance harmonizes with the parables of "The Talents" and "The Pounds" and they in turn are identical in their teaching. Both refer to a man of social rank and financial standing about to travel to a distant land. According to St. Matthew, he entrusts three of his bondservants with five talents, two talents, and one talent respectively. St. Luke mentions ten bondservants, but as Jesus never crowds His stage, only three are prominent in the narrative. The main difference between the two parables is that in St. Matthew's each man receives an amount corresponding to his business ability; whereas in St. Luke's each man receives the same amount. All alike are expected to invest their lord's capital in remunerative enterprises and conserve it until his return.

The law of climax prevails throughout the narratives to bring out the variant characters of the bondservants; especially the strange behavior of the sus-

picious and timid one who wrapped his pound in a
napkin and buried it in the earth. Yet such conceal-
ment was not unusual; and to a superficial view it
seems to have been inspired here by an excess of cau-
tion. Why then did Jesus, who was so sparing in His
adjectives, put into the mouth of the bondservant's
master such strong epithets? Though apparently
nothing worse than stupid and non-productive, this
man is excoriated as "wicked," "slothful" and "unprofitable"; terms signifying a godless person, worm-
eaten with malice, dilatory, careless and entirely without
initiative. The surgeon of the mind requires a surer
eye and a steadier hand than the surgeon of the body.
Christ excelled in both capacities. He sounded the
abysses of the most subtle and complex heart with
swift and delicate perception. His diagnosis of the
unprofitable bondservant was verified by the torrent
of repressed hate and jealousy which leapt from his
diseased mind. The resentment that had burned the
more savagely in him because he had been forced
to hide his emotions, now suddenly exploded. This
supposedly taciturn and retiring individual was ex-
posed as a rank egoist, jealous of better brains than his
own: one for whom loyalty and diligence were no more
than painted words. When under pressure he chose
to bury his pound, afterwards hurling defiance at his

lord, and libelling him to his face as a fraudulent oppressor. He turned on the benefactor who had given him the chance of his life and assailed him with a tirade of villification and lies.

Persons of no conspicuous mentality are often prone to sourness of soul. The rancid outlook of second raters besotted by conceit has created many grave difficulties. Beware of weak men in high office! They charge the consequences of their own folly upon anybody except themselves. The parables also permit the inference that neither massiveness nor mediocrity of mind is a criterion of character. The number of pounds or of talents which God entrusts to us is entirely subordinate to *the motives* that animate our stewardship. If all the evils wrought by ordinary people were balanced against those traceable to virtuosos and celebrities, who can say which would outweigh the other? Again, shy from it as we may, the burden of humanity's progress rests on the shoulders of the one pound man. The ordinary citizen himself is the primal source of betterment in every realm. His diligence and fidelity create that righteous public opinion to which rulers and statesmen must bow. Had this vindictive bondservant realized that life lived on any plane is God's priceless gift, he would have shared the reward of his associates. But he forgot that from Plato and St.

Paul to the veriest dullard, all men are stewards of
what they have received, and that none can discharge
his stewardship save himself. So he forfeited the joy
which rings through the closing scenes of this narrative
like the sound of the opening of the gates of Paradise.

IV. THE PARABLE OF THE FOOLISH FARMER

"And he spake a parable unto them, saying, The ground of a certain rich man brought forth plentifully: and he reasoned within himself, saying, What shall I do, because I have not where to bestow my fruits? And he said, This will I do: I will pull down my barns, and build greater; and there will I bestow all my grain and my goods. And I will say to my soul, Soul, thou hast much goods laid up for many years; take thine ease, eat, drink, be merry. But God said unto him, Thou foolish one, this night is thy soul required of thee; and the things which thou hast prepared, whose shall they be? So is he that layeth up treasure for himself, and is not rich toward God."

St. Luke 12 : 16–21.

IV

As a rule, Jesus used economy of characterization throughout His sayings. Content to portray with gripping fidelity the diversified likenesses of the men and women who appear in His stories, He left His hearers to form their own judgments and draw their own conclusions. But this parable, and also those of "The Two Builders" and "The Ten Virgins," are exceptions. In all three the persons involved are described as foolish; and a fool, as Christ conceives the type, is a man so utterly absorbed in the immediate and the present as to be entirely oblivious to the distant and the future. On the other hand, the wise man so orders his life that he can say: "tomorrow, do thy worst, for I have lived today." Grave contingencies do not catch him napping! death itself finds him alert, vigilant, intent upon those spiritual capacities for immortality without which it may be forfeited.

Here, for instance, was a farmer whose skill and industry had made him rich. His crops were the envy and admiration of the countryside: none of his competitors could boast of such prolific harvests. One evening, after a busy day spent in his fields, he is overheard soliloquizing: "By building bigger barns I can store this grain, and on its profits in a favorable market, I shall take my ease for many a year to come. I will say to my soul . . . eat, drink, and be merry." But no sooner had he thus resolved, than he heard the mysterious yet imperative voice which said to him: "Thou foolish one, this night is thy soul required of thee." The edifice of his gorgeous dreams was shattered at a blow. His bulging barns and hoarded wealth were of no more aid to his future fate than "Merrie England" was to Elizabeth, its greatest Queen, when, dying, she vainly clung to her departing scepter.

In the Master's judgment, the accumulation of money solely for self-indulgence is an unworthy pursuit. Not that He felt any animus against wealth itself. But its inherent grossness had to be transmuted by spiritual chemistries into benevolence and service before it could contribute to the soul's true endowment. St. Paul's assertion that, though a pauper in this world's goods, he was the disburser of untold moral affluence to many; though penniless, he nevertheless possessed all things, is sanctioned by Christ's teaching. The Apostle, as one of God's notable millionaires, had in mind treasures foreign to this opulent yet beggared farmer's thought. For the covetousness which is idolatry had destroyed his moral fiber, and left him a bankrupted soul in the moment of approaching death. Besides, he had been made rich by the toil of others. The ploughmen and vinedressers of his great estate were essential factors in his struggle for material success. Yet he did not give them a passing thought when debating what he should do with his money. His avowal that he had no place to bestow his goods condemned his selfishness out of his own mouth. Were there no ruined homes to rebuild, no broken lives to mend, no hungry and naked supplicants to feed and clothe? Of course there were. Palestine was cursed with an apparently irremediable poverty. But this shortsighted plutocrat heeded nothing and nobody save his riches, and when he vanished, they vanished for him. A fool he was, and he went to his own place. There we may leave him to the mercy of God. But what of the myriads in this more enlightened time who pattern after him, and insist that his policy is the sagacious one? What indeed!

V. THE PARABLE OF THE SHREWD STEWARD

"And he said also unto the disciples, There was a certain rich man, who had a steward; and the same was accused unto him that he was wasting his goods. And he called him, and said unto him, What is this that I hear of thee? render the account of thy stewardship; for thou canst be no longer steward. And the steward said within himself, What shall I do, seeing that my lord taketh away the stewardship from me? I have not strength to dig; to beg I am ashamed. I am resolved what to do, that, when I am put out of the stewardship, they may receive me into their houses. And calling to him each one of his lord's debtors, he said to the first, How much owest thou unto my lord? And he said, A hundred measures of oil. And he said unto him, Take thy bond, and sit down quickly and write fifty. Then said he to another, And how much owest thou? And he said, A hundred measures of wheat. He saith unto him, Take thy bond, and write fourscore. And his lord commended the unrighteous steward because he had done wisely: for the sons of this world are for their own generation wiser than the sons of the light. And I say unto you, Make to yourselves friends by means of the mammon of unrighteousness; that, when it shall fail, they may receive you into the eternal tabernacles."

St. Luke 16 : 1–9.

V

THIS parable has evoked the scorn of skeptics and troubled the conscience of believers. The spectacle of a dishonest agent who was loudly generous with his master's funds is at first glance exceedingly depressing. He threw several anchors to windward in full view of the onrushing storm raised by his roguery, and in so doing did not hesitate to plunge still deeper into chicanery and plunder. Learned scholars have exercised considerable ingenuity in their endeavors to explain the narrative. Some insist that it could not have come from the lips of Jesus. Others maintain that while it is His utterance in part, it teaches as a whole principles unworthy of One "whose words were always like Himself—noble, generous, unworldly." Certainly it is safe to say that Christ's general instruction forbids the idea that He would justify, even for laudable purposes, the slightest taint of fraud and corruption; or in any way indorse these vices.

But if verses eight, nine and ten of the parable are regarded as the interpolations of later scribes, its difficulties disappear, and its bold challenge for the consecration of wealth resounds throughout the abbreviated narrative. The eighth verse may be taken to mean that not Jesus, but the agent's master, commended him for exhibiting more sagacity and foresight than "the children of light." This is precisely what Jesus never did. On the contrary, as in the parable of "The Two Builders," he extolled "the children of light" for their prudence in preparing for future events. The Greek term which Dr. Moffatt's version translates "looking ahead," is used of the wise builder's prevision; and also of the five wise virgins who took oil in their lamps as well as their vessels when they went to meet the belated Bridegroom. Nor are "the children of this world" disposed to think seriously about the future. Reproached by their past and menaced by what is to come, they naturally take refuge in the present. Dr. Moffatt renders the ninth verse as follows: "I tell you, use mammon, dishonest as it is, to make friends for yourselves, so that when you die, they may welcome you to the eternal abodes." This saying, again, is opposed to the whole body of Christ's doctrine, and it bears all the marks of an inferior origin. That shorn of its excrescences the parable insisted on the right use of wealth is patent from what comes next. Its extension in verses ten to thirteen includes genuine sayings of Jesus. Assuredly "no servant can serve two masters: for either he will hate the one and love the other: or else he will hold to the one and despise the other. Ye cannot serve God and mammon." The Pharisees, who loved their money, scoffed at those pronouncements. But would they have done so had Jesus openly indorsed the shrewd steward's disreputable behavior? Moreover, the verses named as of doubtful authorship are foreign to the parable's purpose. It advises us, when read apart from them, that absolute integrity in all financial matters is a requisite discipline of life which qualifies us for the possession of the "true riches" of God's Kingdom.

CHAPTER VI
PARABLES OF MORAL INSTRUCTION
AND WARNING
(CONTINUED)

I. THE PARABLE OF DIVES AND LAZARUS

"Now there was a certain rich man, and he was clothed in purple and fine linen, faring sumptuously every day: and a certain beggar named Lazarus was laid at his gate, full of sores, and desiring to be fed with the crumbs that fell from the rich man's table; yea, even the dogs came and licked his sores. And it came to pass, that the beggar died, and that he was carried away by the angels into Abraham's bosom: and the rich man also died, and was buried. And in Hades he lifted up his eyes, being in torments, and seeth Abraham afar off, and Lazarus in his bosom. And he cried and said, Father Abraham, have mercy on me, and send Lazarus, that he may dip the tip of his finger in water, and cool my tongue; for I am in anguish in this flame. But Abraham said, Son, remember that thou in thy lifetime receivedst thy good things, and Lazarus in like manner evil things: but now here he is comforted, and thou art in anguish. And besides all this, between us and you there is a great gulf fixed, that they that would pass from hence to you may not be able, and that none may cross over from thence to us. And he said, I pray thee therefore, father, that thou wouldest send him to my father's house; for I have five brethren; that he may testify unto them, lest they also come into this place of torment. But Abraham saith, They have Moses and the prophets, let them hear them. And he said, Nay, father Abraham: but if one go to them from the dead, they will repent. And he said unto him, If they hear not Moses and the prophets, neither will they be persuaded, if one rise from the dead."

St. Luke 16 : 19–31.

Chapter VI

PARABLES OF MORAL INSTRUCTION AND WARNING (*Continued*)

I

THE poet who to purity of feeling and range of imagination adds the supreme gift of expression is a revealer of divine verities. He enables his fellow men and women to see things as they are and to apprehend what they contain. Their content is not put in them, but drawn out of them by his more steadfast vision and poignant sympathy. We have ventured to speak of Jesus as God's poet; and if any parable of His justifies this title more than another, it is that of "Dives and Lazarus." Observe its masterly use of contrast, which is also stamped on His other stories. Dives is luxuriously housed and clothed. His residence is a palace crowded with parasites and lackeys who wait on his nod. Its lofty corridors and halls are filled with whatever enchants the eye, and gratifies the tastes of the wealthy and the powerful. Every day is loaded for him with delights that pall. He has magnificent banquets, but no appetite to eat them. He is enveloped in a moral fog, so that Lazarus he sees not at all, or if he does, he may as well not have seen him, for his chariots and outriders pass the destitute beggar at the palace gates without stopping. Yet every sore on that beggar's body had in it a tongue to proclaim his woes; every rag that revealed rather than covered his nakedness challenged Dives' purple and fine linen. While Lazarus solicited the crumbs from the millionaire's table, the stray dogs which were his only friends crept up and licked his sores.

Then came the great Leveller; just and mighty Death, and five minutes after the rich man and the beggar had obeyed his mandate, their situations were reversed. Dives suffered anguish and torment in Hades, the abode of departed spirits, and Lazarus was lodged in Abraham's bosom, the sacred shrine of the Jewish paradise. We must not treat too literally the Master's concrete allusions to life beyond the grave, since He adapted His imageries to the traditional beliefs of the time. He also brought in the Eastern custom of carrying beggars to the likeliest places for their relief by the charitable. Even today a syndicate exists in Calcutta which organizes its thousands of mendicants and directs them to the most advantageous begging stations. This, again, is the only parable of Jesus which *names* the persons implicated. Though

Dives' character is not stressed in the picture, his actions reveal it. Plainly he was a jaded lover of self and pleasure who lived, in so far as he lived at all, for his own gratification, and was indifferent to human suffering, even in its acute stages. His misused wealth and the dire need of the helpless Lazarus permit the inference that Jesus implicitly condemned such an unequal distribution of this world's goods. Any society cursed with acquisitiveness, excess, snobbery and brutality at the one end, and poverty's degrading evils at the other, is diametrically opposed to the mind of the Master and the purpose of God.

But Jesus went beyond the lights and shadows of human life, and showed that a man's social status here is no guarantee of what it shall be hereafter. Earthly prosperity was a patent proof for the Pharisees of its owner's favorable standing with the Deity. They believed that the wealthy and the great in this life would be wealthy and great in that which is to come. The belief is native to the Orient. The tombs and monoliths of its dead monarchs are covered with carvings which convey the idea that they spend eternity as they had spent time, in victorious expeditions of war, and trampling on the necks of their enemies. Jesus demolished this prevalent notion; but He did not teach that heaven is reserved for those who have failed on earth. He warned the revelers of His day and of ours that the inhumanities of the godless rich are an abomination to the God of justice and of brotherhood. Those who practice them do so at their peril, since they cleave an impassable chasm between themselves and their future blessedness.

Dives showed he was capable of better things by his plea that his five brothers should be warned of his doom. Its rejection was based upon adequate grounds. Everything necessary for a man's spiritual deliverance is around and within him. The redemptive forces which make the profligate clean, the miser generous, the proud humble, and the liar truthful, are always active. What those forces have achieved in the past, they can achieve now. Not one has been withdrawn from the service of mankind. But they should be enlisted at once. Let us beware of asking for more time: misfortune seldom grants it. Now is the accepted moment: now is the day of salvation!

II. THE PARABLE OF THE PHARISEE AND THE PUBLICAN

"Two men went up into the temple to pray; the one a Pharisee, and the other a publican. The Pharisee stood and prayed thus with himself, God, I thank thee, that I am not as the rest of men, extortioners, unjust, adulterers, or even as this publican. I fast twice in the week; I give tithes of all that I get. But the publican, standing afar off, would not lift up so much as his eyes unto heaven, but smote his breast, saying, God, be thou merciful to me a sinner. I say unto you, This man went down to his house justified rather than the other: for every one that exalteth himself shall be humbled; but he that humbleth himself shall be exalted."

St. Luke 18 : 10–14.

II

THE splendor of the Master's righteous anger has
been glossed over by writers who distrust the illimitable
sweep of His wholly inspired mind. He hated sin because He loved the sinner it destroyed. And if His
condemnation of pharisaical pride, immorality and
obscurantism was severe, its severity was prompted
by the fact that these offenses of the spirit were far
more fatal than those of the flesh. Therefore on them
he waged a truceless war. Praying Pharisees who
never really prayed were a public spectacle in Jerusalem and other cities and towns of Palestine. Since
they prayed "within" themselves, and packed their
references with personal eulogies delivered openly,
such petitions ended where they began. They could
not break away from the fond conceits which encased
them. Consider in this relation the Pharisee of the
parable. He disqualified himself for an approach to
God by his insufferable pride. Embedded in the sense
of his superiority, he brazenly announced that he was
not as "the rest of men, extortioners, unjust, adulterers,
or *even as this publican*." He was entirely correct
about his unlikeness to the publican, but he would

145

have been astounded could he have known wherein the difference lay. Jesus made it plain. The publican may not have fasted twice a week, nor have given tithes of all he possessed. But he had the indispensable qualities of a true supplicant. Convinced of his own unworthiness, sad and self-reproachful by reason of his sinfulness, unable to lift his eyes upward in the extremity of his penitence, he could only beat his breast, and send to Heaven the most moving petition that ever came from a contrite soul: "God be merciful to me a sinner!" We are told that "he went down to his house justified rather than the other." Quite so! but the question arises: why did the presumptuous Pharisee pray at all? Surely one as whole as he felt himself to be needed no physician, but those who are sick of self and sin, and who stoop themselves to save.

This the tax gatherer did, and brief as his cry for God's compassion was, it embraced the three vital elements of prayer. First, *he was reverent*. His sense of the majestic creativeness of the Eternal Father shone like a jewel in his soul. Upon entering the Temple, he stood "afar off," and there heard, as Isaiah of old had heard, the seraphic voices crying: "Holy, Holy, Holy, is Jehovah of hosts: the whole earth is full of his glory."[1] Offered in this spirit his

[1] Isaiah 6 : 3.

prayer surmounted all obstacles, and he secured an immediate audience with the Lord. Again, *he was humble*. His words were sanctified by that beautiful grace of humility which blooms in the garden of Christ. It bespeaks the soil in which it grows. The word itself is derived from the Latin term "humus"—the ground. The publican remained on "terra firma"; the giddy heights of arrogance and self-assertion did not allure him. He prostrated himself in the dust from which the God who heard and answered him fashioned the first man. Finally, *he was aware of his desperate state*. It aroused in him that longing for forgiveness which should suffuse every prayer. These three qualities exist in the prayer which is the Christian's vital breath, his native air, his watchword at the gates of death, and his means of entrance into life hereafter.

III. THE PARABLE OF THE FRIEND AT MIDNIGHT

"And he said unto them, Which of you shall have a friend, and shall go unto him at midnight, and say to him, Friend, lend me three loaves; for a friend of mine is come to me from a journey, and I have nothing to set before him; and he from within shall answer and say, Trouble me not: the door is now shut, and my children are with me in bed; I cannot rise and give thee? I say unto you, Though he will not rise and give him because he is his friend, yet because of his importunity he will arise and give him as many as he needeth."

St. Luke 11 : 5–8.

148

III

IN St. Luke's Gospel this parable of the persistent
friend occurs immediately after the shorter form of the
Lord's Prayer (11 : 1–4), which covers the honoring
of God's Name, the advance of His Kingdom, the
supply of our daily bread and the forgiveness of our
sins. Thus informed of the content of prevailing
prayer, we gather from the context what should be its
spirit. Jesus asks who among his hearers would fail
to observe the honored rites of hospitality, even though
these demanded extraordinary measures? For example, an Oriental is unexpectedly visited at a late
hour by one of his friends, who solicits food and shelter
while journeying far from his own home. But there is
no food in the house to set before this hungry and tired
traveler. In his dilemma the distracted host hastily
casts about, and remembers a near neighbor whose
larder is always well supplied. Although it is now
midnight, he arouses him, states his difficulty, listens
to the neighbor's excuses, pays no heed to them, and
ultimately, through sheer pertinacity, succeeds in ob-
taining the desired help. Likewise, prayers for God's
blessing which are motivated by heartfelt need are in-

woven with sincerity. "Save, Lord, or I perish!"
has in it the essence of a score of lovely liturgies. Its
impetus never fails to reach heaven, whereas conventional and lifeless petitions stay where they start
—on earth. The story insists that the spiritual elements of prayer must be assiduously cultivated if
they are to conquer personal or social evils. Christians
who go out to win converts cannot succor their distress, nor be considerate and loving toward the erring
and the unlovable, unless they themselves demand
until they get God's living bread for the soul. If the
religious forces of Christendom are to make their inward resistance superior to every outward pressure,
constant, unremitting supplication must batter down
every door of opportunity now closed against those
forces. Otherwise, our institutional methods will sink
to a naturalistic level, and the prayerless believer be
indistinguishable from the actual worldling. The redemptive passion Jesus thrust into human life is fed
and kept vigorous for every needed sacrifice by unremitting prayer to the Father of lights, "who giveth
to all liberally and upbraideth not."[1]

[1] James 1 : 5.

IV. THE PARABLE OF THE IMPORTUNATE WIDOW

"And he spake a parable unto them to the end that they ought always to pray, and not to faint, saying, There was in a city a judge, who feared not God, and regarded not man: and there was a widow in that city: and she came oft unto him, saying, Avenge me of mine adversary. And he would not for a while: but afterward he said within himself, Though I fear not God, nor regard man; yet because this widow troubleth me, I will avenge her, lest she wear me out by her continual coming. And the Lord said, Hear what the unrighteous judge saith. And shall not God avenge his elect, that cry to him day and night, and yet he is longsuffering over them? I say unto you, that he will avenge them speedily. Nevertheless, when the Son of man cometh, shall he find faith on the earth?"

St. Luke 18 : 1–8.

IV

THE impious and unjust judge who figures in this parable met his match in a widow, outraged by the flagrant wrongs she suffered, and bound to get rid of them. She camped on his crooked trail, and like "the man from Shropshire" in "Bleak House," insisted on being heard at any time and in any place. At last he yielded to her importunity, not because he felt a spasm of justice, but lest his personal ease and the emoluments of his office should be further risked. The Greek term translated here as "troubleth" literally means to give a person a black eye, or to beat him till he is discolored. It occurs again in the first Epistle to the Corinthians,[1] and is rendered in our versions as "buffet," viz.: to strike with the hand, contend with, and oppose blow to blow. It is primarily an athletic word belonging to the pugilistic arena. Jesus must have used a very strong corresponding Aramaic term to convey His absolute requirement of importunity in prayer. The foregoing parable upon "The Friend at Midnight" refers to energetic intercession for physical needs. This parable brings in a defenseless woman bent on the redress of her grievances by a polluted jurist.

[1] I Corinthians 9 : 27.

With Cassandra, the unregarded Trojan prophetess of ill, fated to prophesy truly, yet to be rejected, the heroic widow could aver in her desolation that though she had lost much, she still possessed her own soul. Having that, and a righteous cause, she overcame the despicable magistrate. The human interest of the widow's situation stresses Christ's teaching on effective prayer.

Importunity alone, however, is not sufficient. The great prayer which has ploughed itself into the world's heart comes from beneath the gray olive trees of Gethsemane's garden. There the agonizing Redeemer importuned His Father that the cup should be removed from Him. But in His own holy way He qualified the request with the words: "not my will, but thine, be done."[1] The parable of the importunate widow closes with the significant question: "Nevertheless, when the Son of man cometh, shall he find faith on the earth?"[2] Does not Jesus here solicit that faith in God's willingness to answer prayer: prayer which pleads His gracious promises with determination and purpose, because the supplicants are assured that He will equip them for the Holy War, and vouchsafe them the victory which overcomes the world?

[1] St. Luke 22 : 42.   [2] St. Luke 18 : 8.

V. THE PARABLE OF THE LIGHTED LAMP AND
THE GIRDED LOIN

"Let your loins be girded about, and your lamps burning; and be ye yourselves like unto men looking for their lord, when he shall return from the marriage feast; that, when he cometh and knocketh, they may straightway open unto him. Blessed are those servants, whom the lord when he cometh shall find watching: verily I say unto you, that he shall gird himself and make them sit down to meat, and shall come and serve them. And if he shall come in the second watch, and if in the third, and find them so, blessed are those servants. But know this, that if the master of the house had known in what hour the thief was coming, he would have watched, and not have left his house to be broken through. Be ye also ready: for in an hour that ye think not the Son of man cometh."

St. Luke 12 : 35–40.

V

THE lamp is nearly as old as the race. Its various kinds have been dug out of the débris of towns and cities lost in the dim legends of the past. From their age to this, and within the recollection of many of our older generation, the lighting of the lamp at eventide was a distinct domestic event. Every household had memories connected with its soft warm glow, which fell on forms and faces "loved long since, and lost awhile." The numerous allusions in literature to the lamp testify to its importance. How frequently the examined and prepared life is compared to a lamp trimmed and burning, and nowhere so impressively as in the Bible. Jeremiah, in his pathetic description of the national chaos about to descend upon Israel, laments that there will be no light of the lamp in her villages.[1] Jesus, in the Sermon on the Mount, elects His followers to be God's candles, and adjures them to let their light shine before men.[2] He presupposes in the most obscure and backward members of our race a kinship with His Father similar to that which the

[1] Jeremiah 25 : 10.   [2] St. Matthew 5 : 14–16.

157

candle has with the sun. Civilization's winding path
down the centuries has been irradiated by Jesus and
those who shone in His light. The darkness which
would ensue if that light were withdrawn is inconceiv-
able. It shone on Rome in her decadence and it shines
on the world we know as it never shone before. St.
Paul bore it aloft in apostolic Christianity; St. Augus-
tine in patristic Christianity; St. Francis in mediæval
Christianity; Luther in the Christianity of the Refor-
mation, and Wesley in that of the Georgian age. Lamps
of the Lord never shed a more grateful light than that
which they have cast upon the sick, the sorrowful and
the despairing. Was not Florence Nightingale called
"the lady with the lamp"? Hosts of the "illuminati"
who preceded and followed her have rescued those
who sat in darkness and in the shadow of death. The
girdle was almost as essential for the household's
wardrobe as the lighted lamp was for its welfare. The
warrior and the worker alike depended on the girdle
to tighten their armor or to gather in their flowing
robes. The Israelites on the march from bondage to
freedom were enjoined to speed their movements by
using the girdle. Its metaphorical meaning is closely
related to discipline, alertness, and above all, to service. At the Last Supper Jesus took a towel and having
girded Himself with it, washed His disciples' feet.

St. Paul adopted the girdle as the symbol of his servitude. A slave of Christ, forever linked to Him, the Apostle was thereby God's freeman. The vigilance these illustrations teach is amplified in the next parable.

VI. THE PARABLE OF THE WISE AND FOOLISH VIRGINS

"Then shall the kingdom of heaven be likened unto ten virgins, who took their lamps, and went to meet the bridegroom. And five of them were foolish, and five were wise. For the foolish, when they took their lamps, took no oil with them: but the wise took oil in their vessels with their lamps. Now while the bridegroom tarried, they all slumbered and slept. But at midnight there is a cry, Behold, the bridegroom! Come ye forth to meet him. Then all those virgins arose, and trimmed their lamps. And the foolish said unto the wise, Give us of your oil; for our lamps are going out. But the wise answered, saying, Peradventure there will not be enough for us and you: go ye rather to them that sell, and buy for yourselves. And while they went away to buy, the bridegroom came; and they that were ready went in with him to the marriage feast: and the door was shut. Afterward came also the other virgins, saying, Lord, Lord, open to us. But he answered and said, Verily I say unto you, I know you not. Watch therefore, for ye know not the day nor the hour."

St. Matthew 25 : 1–13.

160

VI

THOSE ancient days when Jesus taught were unquiet, thick with blows, turbulence and subterfuge. His antagonists cozened the people until He came and stirred their hearts to a new, warm, human faith which brought God into their lives. The two groups for and against the Master could not be avoided by Him. They appear in nearly all His parables, and these set them forth in their various moods and aspects. In addition to emphasizing the well lit lamp this sequential story insists on its requisite reserves of oil. The wise virgins recognized the need of the provision, the foolish ones trusted to the run of events. All the ten desired a part in the wedding feast; but those who relied on chance were shut out, while those who excluded chance were admitted. They met at the bride's house, where they lit their lamps, and then went to meet the bridegroom, expecting his arrival at a given time and place. But he was delayed, so they turned aside to a nearby resting place, and wearied with their night journey, fell asleep. At last the cry arose that he drew near, whereupon they joined the festive procession to greet him. But they had not gone far before the foolish virgins discovered that their lamps were flickering out for want of oil. The parable describes the outcome of their shortsightedness, and how their companions who had made provision for the unusual reaped the benefit of their wisdom. They find their hearts' desire and the light of the bridal feast falls on them. But the foolish ones are left outside under the dark and cheerless sky.

This explicit story lingers in the memory because it manifests the untold value of reserves of hope and faith for overcoming life's disappointments and difficulties. Every pastor having the cure of souls realizes the difference between those who, when bowed down with sorrow, unhesitatingly fall back upon God's changeless love, and others, who bewildered by their distress, grope in the gray mists of unbelief and despair. What oil is to a burning lamp, the assurance of our Heavenly Father's unfailing goodness and wisdom is to an afflicted heart. Again, this parable and the preceding one concentrate on the supreme quest of life—*the search for Christ*. He is the Bridegroom of every righteous spirit, and in due time He will keep His appointment with the faithful. But the protracted vigil tries out their confidence, and many succumb to the test. Some take refuge in apathy; others in the dogma that He is about to reappear in materialized form, and reign in terror as God's warrior, with garments rolled in blood. Both groups are lacking in that patience which, after the will of God has been done, keeps its doers tranquil in the assurance that every promise of His shall be fulfilled. How many disciples of Jesus have carried nothing but the lanterns of their trust in Him during life's darkest hours. These they waved aloft however impenetrable the gloom around them. When at last their day broke they found themselves at God's right hand, where there are spiritual pleasures forevermore. For us the exhortation peals forth like the midnight cry of the parable: Feed the lamp which burns brightest when all other lights fail.